" It's everyone's job to make sure

I'm alright "

Report of the Child Protection Audit and Review

Scottish Executive
Edinburgh
2002

"It's everyone's job to make sure I'm alright." ————————————————————————————————

Published by the Scottish Executive © Crown Copyright 2002

Reprinted with amendments (Dec) 2002

Further copies of this report are available from

The Stationery Office Bookshop
71 Lothian Road · Edinburgh EH3 9AZ
Tel 0870 606 5566

ISBN 0 7559 0697 7

Astron B28603 12/02

The text pages of this document are produced from 100% elemental chlorine-free, environmentally-preferred material and are 100% recyclable.

Contents

Foreword

The Executive's vision for Scotland's children is

'A Scotland in which every child matters, where every child, regardless of his or her family background, has the best possible start in life.'

All children in Scotland deserve to be cared for and protected from harm and to grow up in a safe environment in which their rights and needs are respected. Unfortunately, not all children are properly cared for or protected and sometimes the environments in which children live are harmful to their development and wellbeing.

Every adult in Scotland has a role in ensuring all our children live safely and can reach their full potential. Parents, whether living with their children or not, have the most important role to play and other family members will contribute greatly to a child's wellbeing. However, even happy children who are well cared for by their families, sometimes need the support of other adults around them, for example, at times of family stress, in the absence of a parent or when playing outside their homes. As children grow and extend their horizons beyond their homes, organisations such as schools and youth groups have a particular role in safeguarding children. They also educate children about risks and how these can be managed.

The aim of this review is to promote the reduction of abuse or neglect of children, and to improve the services for children who experience abuse or neglect. It pays particular attention to the needs of the small number of children whose family or environmental circumstances are so poor that their future wellbeing is placed at serious risk.

The review, which is the subject of this report, represents the widest enquiry yet carried out into child protection in Scotland. It was carried out by a multi-professional team, was based on up-to-date information on the subject, was informed about systems in other countries, was supported by information and views provided by a wide range of agencies and organisations and – not least of all – had the benefit of views expressed by children and young people themselves affected by abuse and neglect.

All the work which has gone into the review has confirmed the progress which has been made in the past decade to improve protection for Scotland's children, particularly:

- the sound legal framework of the Children (Scotland) Act 1995 which places meeting children's needs to the fore;

- the readiness of many services to embrace joint working in order to secure children's welfare; and

- the committed goodwill and sustained efforts of professionals in those services.

But the task of protecting children is never done. There are still persistent and serious problems to be tackled in Scotland, as this report outlines. This is the right time to take the opportunities presented by earlier improvements:

- to boost the performance of agencies which have a major role in protecting children from harm and neglect, not only individually but – since no one holds all the pieces – as partners; and

- to secure much better improvements for children's lives from the extensive efforts and resources which are committed to protecting them from harm.

The recommendations in this report are founded on the findings of the Review and are designed to introduce change and improvements. They are presented as the basis for a realistic action plan to improve the protection of Scotland's children in the next decade.

Angus Skinner
Chief Social Work Services Inspector
Chair of Child Protection Review Steering Group

"It's everyone's job to make sure I'm alright." ————————————————————

Acknowledgements

The case audit and review were undertaken by a multi-disciplinary team comprising education, medicine, nursing, police, Scottish Children's Reporter Administration and social work professionals, with assistance from Scottish Executive analytical services.

We are indebted to a number of colleagues working with children without whom this review would not have been possible.

A major resource has been young people's contributions to our understanding of their experiences. We are particularly grateful to:

- Aberlour Child Care Trust

- Barnardos

- Children First

- Who Cares, Scotland?

- Women's Aid

who undertook interviews with children and young people on our behalf; and to ChildLine Scotland and Children 1st, ParentLine Scotland volunteers and staff who gave considerable time to collecting data for analysis for the review.

We owe thanks to the link officers of those agencies we inspected for organising our programmes so efficiently. We would also like to thank the 439 staff we interviewed, and others whose work we examined, for their assistance with the case audit.

The Consultative Group gave us excellent advice and support throughout the project and helpfully commented on our approach and the findings as they emerged. The Chairs of Child Protection Committees with whom we also consulted offered us helpful comments.

"It's everyone's job to make sure I'm alright."

Executive Summary

The Child Protection Review

This report presents the findings of the Child Protection review. The central part of the review was an audit of the practice of police, medical, nursing, social work, Scottish Children's Reporter Administration, and education staff. The audit was based on a sample of 188 cases which covered the range of possible concerns about children from early identification of vulnerability to substantiated abuse or neglect.

The views of children and young people, parents and the public have contributed to the findings of the Child Protection Review which are outlined in this report. Eleven children were interviewed as part of the case audit and a further 21 children and young people with experience of the child protection system were interviewed by voluntary organisations. We included the views of 217 children and young people who discussed their experiences and concerns with ChildLine Scotland. Parents were interviewed in the audit in relation to 17 children. In addition, the findings have been informed by the views of 100 parents and other members of the public who rang ParentLine Scotland. A study of public views of child protection also contributed to the findings as did the large consultation exercise which involved parents, the public and professionals.

A literature review, analysis of child protection guidance, analysis of deaths of looked after children and information provided by speakers at a conference on child protection in other countries also informed the review.

This report outlines the findings. It presents recommendations which are based upon these findings. The recommendations are aimed at reducing child abuse and neglect in Scotland and improving services for the children who experience abuse and neglect.

The findings of the review

The circumstances of abused and neglected children

The review found that children experience very serious levels of hurt and harm and live in conditions and under threats that are not tolerable in a civilised society. Many children in the case audit and those who phoned ChildLine Scotland were experiencing serious physical abuse and sexual assault. Some children had been suffering chronic neglect for many years. Many children in the audit and those who phoned ChildLine had experienced more than one form of abuse or neglect and large numbers were living with parental substance misuse or witnessing domestic abuse on a regular basis. Sibling or peer abuse was a feature of many of the cases in the audit and was reported by many of the children who phoned ChildLine. The review findings indicate that the effects of abuse and neglect are considerable including children getting into trouble, running away from home, becoming pregnant, self harming and attempting suicide.

Protecting children

The review found that some children remained at risk of significant harm even though most children in the audit had been known to agencies for a considerable time and there had been previous referrals for many of them, There were examples of cases where neglect continued for some years and where children or their older siblings had been previously registered as being in need of protection.

Children and young people expressed mixed feelings about whether or not the child protection system had protected them. Some children who took part in the ChildLine study or who were interviewed by voluntary agencies said they were glad they had told someone about the abuse and that they now felt protected. Some children said they felt protected now they were in foster or residential care. Other children said they were more vulnerable after reporting abuse or that their position was no different. One of the reasons why some felt that the system had not protected them was because the person who had abused them had not been prosecuted. Similar views were also expressed by parents and children participating in the audit and callers to ParentLine. A small proportion of children felt they were not protected in residential care. They indicated that although they had been taken away from the person who abused them they were now vulnerable to other risks. The analysis of the deaths of looked after children indicated that in some cases agencies might have done more to protect the children who subsequently died.

The audit identified occasions when social work did not take action in response to concerns raised by health visitors and education staff who often perceived that their referrals were not taken seriously enough by social work.

Emergency protection measures were used only rarely in the sample of cases which were looked at. Social workers were reluctant to apply for Child Protection Orders unless they could demonstrate immediate risk to a child and in some cases they were concerned about appearing in court and being cross examined about their work. Other agencies were reluctant to seek an order if social work did not think one was necessary. Social workers felt there was little point in seeking exclusion orders which placed responsibility on the other adult in the household to keep the abuser out.

In some cases children were at serious risk from males who were not living in the family home but who visited the house or lived close by. In such cases Reporters had difficulty framing grounds and the hearing system was not an effective way of protecting the child. In other cases children remained at risk due to delays in the hearings system. There were delays when cases went to the sheriff court for proof; delays were also caused by late presentation of reports by social workers.

Meeting needs

The review found that children and their families do not always get the help they need when they need it. Most of the abuse and neglect experienced by children in the audit was caused by poor parenting skills and agencies responded with a range of compensatory measures to improve the day-to-day conditions for children. There was evidence of high levels of home support stabilising situations, particularly where there were problems of substance misuse. In some cases parents were greatly assisted in developing the ability to care effectively for their children. Where support to improve parenting skills was offered the contributions of family centres or nurseries were particularly impressive and in a few cases health visitors played a significant part.

Examples of meeting need included the provision of therapeutic services where children had an opportunity to work through what happened to them, come to terms with it and move towards a different future; remedial health care to address neglected problems, for example, optical or dental treatment; information and guidance about inappropriate behaviour; and change programmes that targeted entrenched problem behaviours.

In too many cases, however, the audit found that children were not receiving the services they needed and many could not access services such as health care if their parents did not co-operate. Where intensive remedial work was provided solely in the home there was little evidence of long-term success. In some cases children were living at home but virtually all the day-to-day and occasional night care was provided by a range of support services rather than by the parents. In reality the local authority was parenting the child.

A few authorities provided directly or commissioned therapeutic support from voluntary agencies and where these were offered they were valued and made a good contribution to the welfare of the children. On the whole, however, there was a shortage of skilled workers with time to offer children practical and emotional support and psychology, psychiatry and specialist counselling waiting lists were so long that children could not gain access in a reasonable timescale. Some of the parents who called ParentLine were frustrated that they could not access counselling services for children or themselves. The audit found that the needs of child perpetrators were particularly neglected, few of those in the sample had the benefit of a programme to address their sexually abusive behaviour.

The audit found that while professionals had children's 'best interests' at heart, they often did not consult with children to determine what their 'best interests' were. The views of children were often not fully considered at case conferences or were presented through third parties. Children who were interviewed by voluntary agencies complained that they were not always listened to.

The audit found examples where parents valued highly the support they were given. Some parents in the audit and those who rang ParentLine often felt they were not kept fully enough informed about what was happening. Some felt overwhelmed at case conferences. Arrangements to provide families with support were variable as was practice in ensuring they fully understood the outcomes of the meeting. Sometimes key family members, such as grandparents, were omitted from discussions. Relatives who took on the long-term care of children often felt unsupported and felt their requests for help were ignored.

Conclusions

The review findings suggest that many adults and children have little confidence in the child protection system and are considerably reluctant to report concerns about abuse or neglect. Many children never tell anyone they are being abused. The child protection system cannot help these children because they never enter the system and do not receive any help. Many referrals come from members of the public but the findings of the review suggest that the system is not always well understood by the public. The public attitudes study found that many adults were concerned that children would be taken away from their families if they reported abuse. Even where people were willing to report abuse they indicated that gaining access to help was not easy.

The review findings also suggest that the child protection system does not always work well for those children and adults who become involved in it. Forty children in the audit were not protected or their needs were not met following the intervention of agencies. A further 62 children were only partially protected or their needs partially met. In 77 cases children were protected and their needs met and in 24 of these cases their needs were well met.

Good practice included the provision of help to parents and children as and when it was needed, timely responses, early thought and preparation, and properly addressing the source of the risk. Sometimes agencies did all they could but outcomes for children did not improve. While some parents who received considerable support were able to improve their parenting skills and the situation improved for their child(ren), other parents were unable or unwilling to change despite high levels of intervention.

Outcomes for children were found to be highly dependent on social work doing well. Where social work performed well outcomes were generally good and when they performed less well outcomes were generally poor. While good outcomes were assisted by the work of all agencies they were less dependent on other agencies.

Where children were not protected or their needs were not met this was often the result of poor assessments and enquiries which were not sufficiently extensive. Longer-term assessments of risks were often particularly poor. Poor assessments were characterised by failure to consider the pattern of previous events; insufficient use of inter-agency information, especially health and education information; insufficient attention paid to the role of at least one key person in a child's life; lack of focus on the child and inadequate assessment of parents' ability to make use of the support on offer and to change quickly and sufficiently enough to offer children an acceptable level of care.

Practice was generally better for new babies where parents had a learning disability, mental health problem, or drug problem. In such cases health services arranged for pre-birth or pre-discharge meetings with the other key agencies. These worked well when all the key agencies attended, a multi-agency plan was made and the individual workers each played a part in implementing it.

Where, to secure their safety, children were placed successfully in foster care their circumstances, particularly material and health circumstances, often improved. Schools often noted improvements in the attitude and performance of older children following fostering. There were also cases, however, where foster carers could not cope with the behaviour of children. Occasionally children were sent back home from foster or residential placements against their will.

Good workers made a difference to the outcomes for children. In a number of instances, particularly in relation to drugs or alcohol misuse, where strong supportive relationships had been established between social workers and misusing parents, workers were able to address the problems and parents were very positive about the support they received.

Where the child protection system relied on criminal prosecution to protect children outcomes were not always good because the abuser was not always prosecuted or convicted and often remained a threat. In such cases victims were left vulnerable and felt they had not been believed.

Parents do not always feel that the child protection system is working effectively. They are not always happy with the response they receive from child protection agencies. People contacting ParentLine were often concerned about a perceived lack of activity on the part of agencies and felt they received a lack of feedback after making a referral.

The report contains 17 recommendations. The recommendations identify action that can be taken immediately to protect children and improve services as well as action that needs to take place over a longer time scale.

List of Recommendations

Recommendation 1: All agencies should review their procedures and processes and put in place measures – to ensure that practitioners have access to the right information at the right time, and in particular to ensure that:

- Where children present to medical practitioners with an injury or complaint, practitioners must consider what further information is available from their own or other agencies *before they rule out* the possibility of continuing risk.

- Where children present to any hospital, there should be in place mechanisms for checking other health records to ensure a pattern of injuries is not being missed.

- Where there have been concerns about possible abuse or neglect, schools, police, health service and social work service files should contain a succinct, readily accessible chronology of events or concerns which can be easily referred to should a further incident or concern arise. This chronology should contain information relating to the child and, where known, information relating to other people in the child's life, for example, any previous deaths of children of a mother's new partner.

- Courts should ensure bail address suitability checks are undertaken in cases where the alleged offence is against children, or in the case of domestic abuse, where children may be at risk.

- Caldicott guardians in Health Boards and Trusts should ensure that health professionals are aware of their responsibilities towards the care and protection of children. In particular they should ensure that where children are at risk of abuse and neglect information is shared promptly with other relevant professionals in line with the General Medical Council and the Scottish Executive guidance on when medical confidentiality can be breached.

Recommendation 2: Through the Child Protection Committees all agencies should improve access to help for children who have been abused or neglected by:

- providing for single-page contact information for telephone directories, public phones and the web, which identifies local contact points in health services, local authorities, police services, SCRA and the voluntary sector;

- providing for services users and referrers, information about how to access help for children about whom they are worried. This should include information about how and when children and young people will be consulted, what will happen after a referral is made and what, and how, feedback to people who refer concerns will be provided.

Recommendation 3: The Scottish Executive should, in consultation with service providers, draw up standards of practice that reflect children's rights to be protected and to receive appropriate help. All local authorities, health boards, police services and SCRA should undertake regular audits of practice against these standards and report on them annually to the Scottish Executive and local Child Protection Committees.

Recommendation 4: The Scottish Executive should revise the remit of the Child Protection Committees to include:

- Annual auditing and reporting, to constituent agencies and to the Scottish Executive, on the quality of agency and inter-agency work.

- The provision of information to members of the public, volunteers and other professionals.

- Assisting a wider range of organisations to help prevent abuse and neglect through training for staff and volunteers.

- The development of safe recruitment practices for agencies working with young people.

Recommendation 5: Local authority Chief Executives, in consultation with other services, should review the structure, membership and scope of the Child Protection Committee covering their authority and report to their Council and partner agencies on whether it is best constituted to take on the responsibilities for assuring the quality of agency and inter-agency services and the recommendations about their role contained in this report.

Recommendation 6: The Scottish Executive should consult on how child fatality reviews should be introduced in Scotland. This should include consultation on how they should be conducted, how review teams should be constituted, to whom they would report and what legislative framework is required to ensure their effectiveness.

Recommendation 7: The Scottish Executive should strengthen the current arrangements for the development and dissemination of knowledge about abuse and neglect. In particular it should identify:

- the most effective arrangements for recording and collating examples of effective practice;

- the delivery of staff training across all disciplines or agencies;

- the best means of disseminating research findings and best practice; and

- the links between research and knowledge and staff education and training and how this can be consolidated.

Recommendation 8: The Scottish Executive should initiate a long-term study of the effectiveness of current methods of responding to abuse and neglect. The study should follow children from infancy to adulthood.

Recommendation 9: Children's Services Plans should be developed so that they include clear plans for the implementation of national priorities and demonstrate the application of resources to these outcome targets set out in *Building a Better Scotland.*

Recommendation 10: Local authorities' plans for integrated children's services, as the overarching plans and drivers for all local children's services, should develop *positive childhood* initiatives. These should be lead by a children's rights rather than a public service perspective and should promote <u>every</u> child's rights to life, health, decency and development. The Executive should support this with a public campaign.

Recommendation 11: The Scottish Executive should:

- Advise on how agency resources can be pooled and what systems may best be deployed to ensure the most effective joint commissioning of services on behalf of children.

- Commission a study of the costs and benefits of the current child protection system in Scotland and identify costed alternative options for improving outcomes for children.

Recommendation 12: There needs to be a new approach to tackling risks and the needs of the most vulnerable. As a first step this should start with assessment of the needs of all new-born babies born to drug- or alcohol-misusing parents; parents who have a history of neglecting or abusing children and parents where there have been concerns about previous unexplained deaths in infancy. The inter-agency assessment and subsequent action plan in respect of each child should clearly state:

- standards of child care and developmental milestones the child is expected to experience or achieve;

- resources to be provided for the child or to assist the parents in their parenting role; and

- monitoring that will be put into place along with contingency plans should the child's needs fail to be met.

Recommendation 13: In keeping with the philosophy of the Children (Scotland) Act 1995, agencies referring to the Reporter should indicate what action they or their agency has undertaken to achieve change through consent and why compulsory measures of supervision may now be necessary.

Recommendation 14: The Scottish Executive should review the grounds for referral to the Children's Hearing system. Specifically, it should explore the feasibility of grounds being framed to reflect more clearly the needs of the child and to be more closely aligned with definitions of need outlined in the Children (Scotland) Act 1995.

Recommendation 15: In order to meet the shortcomings identified in this report, developing linked computer-based information systems should include a single integrated assessment, planning and review report framework for children in need. For those in need of protection the framework should include reason for concern, needs of the child, plans to meet them and protect them when necessary, and progress since any previous meetings. This core assessment, planning and review framework should be accessible and common to all partner agencies, multi-agency case conferences and the Children's Hearing. Arrangements should be made for appropriate access to information by agencies in other areas should children or their families move.

Recommendation 16: The Scottish Executive in partnership with the regulatory bodies should consult on the minimum standards of professional knowledge and competence required of practitioners who undertake investigations, assessments and clinical diagnosis when working with children and their families. In particular it should establish the minimum necessary qualifications and experience required of those making decisions that fundamentally affect the future wellbeing of children.

Recommendation 17: The Scottish Executive should:

- Establish a national implementation team to take forward the recommendations in the review, in particular the development of standards and local auditing processes.

- Establish a review process for annual reporting on progress and improvements.

- Implement a further national review of child protection in three years' time to be undertaken by a multi-disciplinary inspection team using this report as a baseline against which progress can be assessed.

"It's everyone's job to make sure I'm alright."

Introduction

In Scotland each year, about 10 children are killed by a parent or parent substitute. Following the report by Dr Helen Hammond into the death of one child, Kennedy McFarlane, the (then) Minister for Education, Europe and External Affairs, Jack McConnell, ordered a review of child protection across Scotland. This report presents the findings of the review.

The Work of the Child Protection Review Team

Aims and remit

A multi-disciplinary team was established to carry out this audit and review of child protection. The team included professionals from education, the police, medicine, nursing, the Scottish Children's Reporter Administration and social work. This multi-disciplinary review was able to build on previous multi-disciplinary work, including in particular the multi-disciplinary review of support for vulnerable families which informed the work of the team and is being published simultaneously. The review aimed:

- to promote the reduction of abuse or neglect of children; and

- to improve the services for children who experience abuse or neglect.

The team's remit was:

- To review, throughout Scotland, the practice of medical, nursing, social work, police, Scottish Children's Reporter Administration, education and other public, voluntary and private sector staff to examine how well these:

  - identify those children who may be being abused or neglected;

  - reduce such abuse and neglect;

  - meet these children's needs; and

  - make plans for the future wellbeing of these children.

- To review how well **agencies** work together and public and professional confidence in these services.

- To review how well **professionals** work together and public and professional confidence in the way they work.

- To identify best practice.

- To learn lessons from international developments in this field.

- To report and make recommendations to improve professional working and the regulatory framework within which professionals operate.

The review was managed by a Steering Group chaired by the Chief Social Work Inspector, with representatives from HM Inspectorate of Education, HM Inspectorate of Constabulary, Scottish Executive Health Department, Justice Department and Education Department and the Scottish Children's Reporter Administration. The team was assisted by a consultative group which represented a range of organisations concerned with child protection in Scotland. The group's expertise was essential to the success of the project and regular meetings were held. The team was also supported by the Chairs of the Child Protection Committees and a number of other organisations and individuals were consulted on specific issues which were covered in the review (a full list of people involved in the child protection review can be found in Appendix A).

Methodology

In order to achieve the aims of the review the team set out to answer a number of questions:

- What is the extent of child abuse and neglect in Scotland?
- What help is available to children who have been abused or neglected?
- What help is available to parents and others who care for children?
- What do children and young people, parents, the public and professionals think about the services designed to help or protect children who have been abused and neglected?
- How well are children protected and what is the quality of work?
- What might we learn from other countries?
- How well does the system work?

In order to answer these questions, the review team undertook a range of tasks presented in diagrammatic form in Figure 1. Reports on a number of projects were prepared and some of these are available on the review website: www.scotland.gov.uk/childprotection.

Figure 1: The Child Protection review components

Children 1st ParentLine Study	**Health**
ChildLine Study	**Education**
Messages from young people with experience of the system	**Social Work**
MORI – Public Awareness Study	**Police**
	Reporters
	Interagency
Listening to children, parents and the public	**Fieldwork (188 children)**
	Inspection — **Guidance**

CHILD PROTECTION REVIEW

Child Deaths (Looked after Children)

Literature Review

Lessons from Elsewhere (how other countries protect children)

Statistics

Consultation

Formal Consultation

Consultative Groups

Website

Case audit of practice

Central to this review was a case audit of child protection practice. It included the work of medical, nursing, social work, police, Scottish Children's Reporter Administration, education and other public, voluntary and private sector staff. The field work was carried out between January and March 2002. This multi-agency approach to case audit was new to both the Scottish Executive and those whose work we inspected.

Sampling

We wanted our sample to cover the range of possible concerns about children, from early identification of vulnerability to substantiated abuse or neglect. We asked education, health, police and social work to identify:

- children who had been referred to the police or social work services because of concerns about abuse or neglect in the week beginning 3 September 2001;

- children whose names were on the child protection register on 7 September 2001;

- children whose names were on health visitors' 'cause for concern' lists in the week beginning 3 September 2001; and

- children who had been referred by the education department because of concerns about abuse or neglect in the week beginning 3 September 2001.

In addition, all agencies were given the opportunity to submit one or two cases where they identified particularly good practice.

In total, agencies identified 5,045 cases. We included children on health visitors' 'cause for concern' lists because we wanted our sample to include children about whom agencies had concerns but where these concerns had not necessarily led to child protection referrals. The sheer numbers of children on the health visitor lists (2,666) indicated that health visitors carried a considerable weight of concern about vulnerable children. Only 19 children were referred to social work from education during the identified week.

Although we had included children on health visitors' 'cause for concern' lists, we recognised that we would still miss abused children whose abuse had not yet come to the attention of any statutory agency. It was not possible to consider such children in the case audit but they were included in our ChildLine study which is described below.

From a total sample of 5,045 cases we selected 188 children for in-depth examination across all the agencies involved. To preserve anonymity, agencies were asked to submit only a child identifier unique to the agency. They were also asked to provide date of birth, gender, ethnic origin and the nearest town of residence. This information enabled us to select a sample which reflected the geographical and socio-economic conditions of Scotland and was representative of the age and gender of the childhood population. Particular attention was paid to including cases from the small number of those of black or minority ethnic origin which were submitted.

Inter-agency arrangements

The arrangements for the case audit were made locally by the relevant agencies, and in consultation with each other. We asked that each agency complete a recording document about their involvement with the child and to make available to us, in respect of each child, all the relevant paper work and staff on specified days. The response of different agencies to the task was illustrative of the complexity of inter-agency working and highlighted some of the difficulties. Those involved in the organisation of the visits reflected to us that the process of setting up the interviews and gathering files provided them with insights into their local inter-agency communication and systems for achieving joint tasks.

What we were looking for

We wanted to examine education, health, police, Reporter and social work practice and to assess how well the agencies worked separately and together. The principal focus was on the outcomes for children.

In all 188 cases, we examined detailed information provided by the relevant agencies. In 103 cases we also undertook a detailed examination of case files and conducted interviews with key staff. We carried out in-depth interviews with a total of 438 professionals:

- 136 from social work services;

- 130 from health professions;

- 70 from education;

- 64 from police; and

- 38 Reporters.

In many instances, the same professional was involved with more than one child.

All interviews were structured in the same way so that we would obtain the same information from each and to make the process of analysis easier. Use of the inspection recording document ensured that we were able to record data in chronological order and were also able to give interviewees the opportunity to say what they wanted. Almost all interviews were conducted by pairs of inspectors, with one of the pair being from the discipline being interviewed. The observations we formed from reading the files were also noted on the inspection document. A separate inspection document was filled in for each agency involved in a case.

Introduction

Issues arising during the case audit process

In most of the areas we visited we saw the health files and spoke with the relevant health staff. Often this was at short notice, as health authorities did not always know who the relevant personnel were in respect of each child. Access to health records and staff was affected by the way the issue of confidentiality was interpreted locally. This lead to different approaches:

- records were only available with parental consent;

- health professionals anonymised the records before we saw them;

- health professionals spoke to records and we did not see them;

- no records or interviewees were made available; or

- all records and staff were freely available (the majority of cases).

Overall very few medical staff (GPs and Paediatricians) were available for interview. There was excellent health visitor attendance.

Whether attending school or not, all children of school age are the responsibility of education services. However, in a few authorities, for some children of school age, no arrangements were made for staff to be interviewed or records seen, and we had to request this information. Social work, Reporters and the police knew which staff were involved and were generally able to present both staff and files promptly. All those who attended for interview, of whatever profession or agency, fully co-operated with the team.

All agencies were asked to consider how best to offer families an opportunity to speak to us. Eight local authorities, generally through social workers, made arrangements for such meetings, though some parents and children cancelled the appointments on the day. Eleven children met with us, and a parent or parents spoke to us in relation to 17 children. In some areas, families were not informed of our visit, or given the opportunity to meet with us. Health visitors were unable to approach many of the parents of children on their cause for concern list because either the parents did not know they were on such a list, or if they did, the term 'child protection' had never been used with them.

Evaluation

Once we had looked at files and interviewed professionals we brought all the information together about each child to assess:

- how well each agency had individually met its responsibility to the child; and

- what the overall outcome had been for the child as a result of the efforts of all the agencies.

The review team discussed each case in detail as soon as possible after the interviews had been carried out so that the information remained fresh in our memories. We considered the information contained in the recording and inspection documents and pieced together all the information we had about a particular child. These discussions normally took around two hours and ended with the team rating the performance of each agency according to agreed criteria. The criteria covered both adherence to guidance, but also outcomes for the child. There was a final evaluation of the outcome for the child as a result of the efforts of all the agencies. Cases were described as 'Very Good', 'Strengths Outweighing Weaknesses', 'Weaknesses Outweighing Strengths' or 'Poor'. Very good cases conformed to accepted standards of good practice, the child was protected and their needs were met. At the other extreme, poor cases were those where children remained unprotected and their needs were unmet.

The review team comprised people from a number of different professional backgrounds and experiences. Our expectations of agency behaviour were also different and what was accepted as good practice by one team member might be seen as only adequate or even poor by another. Our discussions about these issues were the cornerstone of our understanding of the findings. It revealed the extent to which there is not a consensus about:

- the best ways of protecting children and who has responsibility for taking action;

- what good communication means; and

- how much sharing of information is appropriate without breaching confidentiality or intruding upon family integrity.

In almost all cases, however, it was possible, through detailed discussion, to arrive at a shared agreement on the overall evaluation of the case. Even where differences of opinion might remain over the individual contribution of agencies to cases, there were few instances where the team were in any doubt about the overall outcome for the child.

Once practice had been scored the information from each case was entered into a database for quantitative analysis. All the demographic details supplied on the recording documents and obtained during the case audit were included. The ratings were also entered so that the database allowed identification of individual cases for more detailed assessment.

The views of children

The review team were very keen to hear children and young people's views on child protection. We recognised, however, that obtaining young people's views on such a sensitive issue would be problematic. It is difficult to carry out research with children and young people, it is especially difficult when the subject is such a distressing one as child abuse and neglect. We told agencies that we wanted to speak to children and young people during the case audit of practice but out of a total sample of 188 children we were only able to speak to 11 (6%). Many children were too young, others did not want to speak to us or agencies did not ask them to take part because they did not feel that it was appropriate.

In anticipation that it would be difficult to talk to young people about such a difficult issue, we developed a number of methods to, cumulatively, ensure the voices of children and young people could be heard.

Messages from young people

We carried out a study in conjunction with five voluntary agencies – Aberlour, Barnardos, Children 1st, Who Cares? Scotland and Women's Aid. These organisations agreed to interview children and young people on our behalf and to pass the information to us for analysis. In recognition of the potential problems of interviewing children and young people we established a number of principles to guide the process including:

- all participants were given a confidentiality statement;

- no young person was asked to recount direct experiences of abuse or neglect;

- all participants were provided with an information letter about the review;

- a young person was able to withdraw from or terminate a discussion at any point;

- a young person was provided with support during and after taking part in the consultation exercise; and

- informed, written consent was obtained from each young person taking part. For young people under 12 and for all young people with a clinically diagnosed learning disability or mental health problem additional written consent was sought from the parents or carers with parental responsibility for the young person. For children over 12, parents were informed of the consultation exercise.

The staff who carried out the interviews received a detailed list of our areas of interest and a checklist for collecting young people's views. The checklist was used flexibly and tailored to the needs of the young person so that the areas of discussion were not restricted and young people were able to comment on any aspect of the child protection system they wished. The areas of interest were:

- Describe the experience of being involved in formal child protection proceedings and what it felt like for you.

- Working through the events, what were the most helpful things that happened?

- Working through the events, what were the most unhelpful things that happened?

- Thinking about all the different people who may have been involved in the investigation/proceedings, was it clear who they were and what their jobs were?

- Are there things that need to change that would improve the situation for other young people going through similar experiences?

- Do you have any other comments or suggestions about what would help to protect children and young people?

Agencies were confident that many young people would be prepared to take part. However, some agencies were able only to interview a small number of children and young people. They found that children did not want to take part, their parents did not want them to take part, support workers did not feel that taking part would be in their interests or investigations were ongoing or court cases pending and interviews, therefore, could not be carried out. Between them the agencies did succeed, however, in carrying out 21 interviews. The information they collected from the interviews was analysed by the review team and a report of the findings was produced. Although the interviews are based on interviews with only 21 young people, we are confident that the findings of this project are similar to those of previous research studies which have spoken to young people about their experiences of the child protection system. We have used direct quotes from the young people who were interviewed to illustrate points made in the report.

ChildLine research

In order to obtain the views of those children and young people who had been abused or neglected but had not necessarily come into contact with child protection agencies we carried out a project with ChildLine Scotland. We undertook an analysis of calls made to them and letters sent to them on the subject of child abuse and neglect. We analysed ChildLine's statistics over a two-year period and also carried out a more qualitative analysis of all the calls (216) and letters (1) which ChildLine Scotland received on abuse issues over a two-week period in November 2001. All the information passed to us was anonymous. Much of the information was in the form of direct quotes from children and young people and some of these quotes have been used to highlight points made in this report. A report of the findings of the analysis of the ChildLine calls was produced by the child protection team.

The views of parents, members of the public and professionals

The review team also wanted to hear parents' and members of the public's views about child protection. Agencies were told that we wanted to speak to families during the case audit of practice but out of our total sample of 188 children we were only able to speak to parents in relation to 17 children (9%). In many instances practitioners judged it inappropriate to contact parents because of the nature of the ongoing circumstances. We were, however, able to obtain further information about parents' views and those of other family members, neighbours, and concerned citizens from the exercise we carried out with ParentLine Scotland.

ParentLine research

Children 1st run a helpline – ParentLine – which is for parents and other adults who have concerns about children and young people. We carried out an analysis of the calls ParentLine receive on the subject of child abuse and neglect in order to find out something about why some people do not choose to contact official agencies about their concerns. It was also expected that some callers would have had experience of contacting child protection agencies and we aimed, therefore, to obtain information about the nature of this contact. We carried out a quantitative analysis of ParentLine Scotland's statistics over a two-year period. We also carried out a more in-depth analysis of 100 calls which ParentLine received on child abuse and neglect over a five-month period dating back from September 2001. The information ParentLine passed to us for analysis was anonymous. Some of the information which callers provided has been used to illustrate points which have been made in this report. The child protection team also produced a report outlining the findings of the analysis of calls to ParentLine.

Public perceptions, understanding and views about child protection in Scotland

MORI Scotland were commissioned to undertake a study to assess:

- levels of public knowledge and understanding of the child protection process;

- expectations about the role of individuals, communities and public agencies in child protection; and

- views about the degree to which they, as members of the public, should take responsibility or become involved.

In November and December 2001 MORI conducted eight focus groups (each comprising eight to 10 people) at a range of locations across Scotland among a cross section of the general public. The discussions focused on the following issues:

- life in today's society;

- awareness of the child protection system;

- scenarios;

- perception of areas of responsibility;

- information needs; and

- key priorities for the Scottish Executive review team.

MORI produced a report of the key findings of this research. Much of the information in the report was in the form of quotes and some of the quotes have been used in this report.

Consultation

The views of the public and professionals were also obtained through a consultation exercise which comprised two principal elements:

- a questionnaire that was circulated to a wide range of statutory and voluntary sector agencies involved with, and concerned about, matters of child protection; and

- a website that was available to members of the general public, including children, to record their views and comments about matters relating to child protection.

A total of 1,219 questionnaires were sent out to:

- Academic bodies 50

- Statutory agencies 801

- Voluntary agencies 222

- Private individuals 17

- MSPs 129.

The website was open from 20 November 2001 to 31 January 2002. The questionnaire and the website were structured around three questions:

- What helps the protection of children?

- What hinders or prevents the protection of children?

- What would improve the wellbeing and protection of children in Scotland?

A total of 110 completed questionnaires were submitted as formal responses on behalf of statutory or voluntary sector agencies, academic institutions or professional bodies that are involved with child protection. A total of 176 individual responses were recorded on the website or on completed questionnaires. An independent analyst provided an analysis of all the responses received from the consultation process and produced a report outlining the key findings of this process.

Other projects

A range of other projects were carried out to inform the work of the review team and to provide further information about child protection:

Lessons from elsewhere

In order to find out more about child protection practice elsewhere an international seminar was held in Edinburgh on 20 March 2002 at which the following speakers informed conference members about the systems in place in Australia, Belgium, Canada, France, Germany and Sweden:

Adam M Tomison	Australian Institute of Family Studies
Professor Andrew Cooper	The Tavistock Clinic and University of East London
Dr Catherine Marneffe	Medical Director of the Paediatric Centre 'Clairs Vallons', France
Evelyn Khoo	Umeå University, Sweden
Lennart Nygren	Umeå University, Sweden;

workshops allowed further discussion of the issues which were raised by the speakers. Professor Malcolm Hill (University of Glasgow) chaired the event and produced a report based on the findings from the seminar. This report can be seen in Appendix B.

Analysis of Guidance

All available national and local inter- and intra-agency guidance on child protection procedures was analysed, as was guidance from the Armed Forces and faith groups. A sample of guidance used by sports clubs was also looked at.

In analysing agency guidance, consideration was given to the layout, tone and accessibility of the guidelines, and to the extent to which various areas were covered. There was a focus on the extent to which the following were covered:

- the legal background;
- the definitions and descriptions of child abuse;
- roles played by the various agencies;

- degree of emphasis on inter-agency working;

- agency or organisation procedures to be followed when a case arose;

- the role of parents;

- involvement of children in the proceedings; and

- additional advice for more complex situations such as abuse of a child with special needs.

Through such an analysis, it was possible to determine the extent to which, within an area, the guidelines used by different agencies were consistent, showed an awareness of possible complexities and promoted:

- a focus on the child's needs;

- partnership with parents; and

- effective inter-agency working.

In looking at the guidance provided by faith groups and sports clubs, particular attention was paid to the readability and clarity of guidance, appointments procedures for staff and volunteers and the degree of emphasis given to referring disclosures of child abuse to the statutory agencies.

Literature review

The literature review was designed to provide an overview of the ideas and research evidence on child abuse and child protection. The research evidence was presented in three parts: definitions and information; identification and assessment; addressing the problem and 'what works'. A wide range of national and international journal articles and publications were consulted in the process of producing the literature review. The literature review is published as an accompaniment to this report.

Deaths of Looked After Children

An analysis of the deaths of the 50 Looked After Children (LAC) who died between April 1997 and December 2001 was undertaken. In the event of a death of a child who is looked after local authorities are required to notify the Minister. Information, obtained from all reports, to the Minister about all children and young people who died between these dates was collated on a database. Information from reports which are notified to the Minister after this date will also be collated on this database and it is anticipated that the database will be used to record and assist the analysis of future reports of deaths of looked after children. A report outlining the findings of the analysis of reports of children who died between April 1997 and December 2001 was produced by the review team.

Deaths of children

National statistics and a range of publications were used to provide an analysis of the deaths of all children in the community. A report was produced which outlined the findings of this analysis.

Legal aspects of child protection

Professor Kathleen Marshall was commissioned to advise on the legal issues for all the agencies involved, surrounding child protection. She produced a paper, which outlined the Scottish and European legal framework for agency decision making, relevant to potential child protection cases.

Statistics

Statisticians from the Scottish Executive Education Department worked closely with the child protection team in order to provide statistical support.

The structure of the report

Chapter 1 provides an overview of current knowledge about child abuse and neglect and its extent.

Chapters 2-4 present the findings of the case audit. Chapter 2 describes the circumstances of the children in the sample. Chapter 3 considers how well the children in the sample were protected and chapter 4 assesses whether their needs were met and what the outcomes for children were.

Chapter 5 considers what leads to success in child protection and discusses the issue of accountability.

Chapter 6 discusses how well the child protection system works according to the views of those who have most need of it – children, parents and members of the public. It draws on the ChildLine Scotland, ParentLine Scotland, messages from young people and MORI studies which were undertaken specifically for the review.

Chapter 7 draws on other elements of the review – the literature review, lessons from elsewhere, deaths of looked after children and consultation responses.

Chapter 8 looks to the future. In the light of the key findings, it sets out what needs to change and makes a number of recommendations which are intended to bring about these changes.

It's everyone's job to make sure I'm alright.

Child Protection

What is child abuse and neglect?

What is child protection?

What is the extent of child abuse and neglect?

The changing social context

Signposts to success

1.1

All children in Scotland are entitled to proper care and protection. Children may need protection when their basic needs such as food and warmth are neglected or they may need protection from harm from other people, the environment or even from themselves.

1.2

Children's lives are like a jigsaw, with different agencies and individuals having responsibility for different pieces. Parents and children themselves tend to hold the largest pieces of the picture. Health visitors and teachers will hold some pieces. For some children, social workers and the police also hold pieces. In this review we wanted to bring all the pieces of the jigsaw together to see the complete picture of children's lives and needs. A number of agencies have specific responsibilities towards children. These include education, health, police, the Scottish Children's Reporter Administration and social work. It is, however, the responsibility of all adults to protect children, hence our title 'It's everyone's job to make sure I'm alright' – the words of one of the young people who participated in the review.

What is child abuse and neglect?

1.3

There is no single agreed definition of what child abuse and neglect is and definitions have changed over time. Abuse can be physical, sexual or emotional. It may be acute or involve a long-term pattern of physical neglect. Often children are abused in more than one way.

1.4

As understanding of child abuse and neglect has increased, situations which are considered to be abusive or neglectful, have broadened to include:

- organised abuse, for example, children involved in prostitution and ritual abuse;

- munchausen's syndrome by proxy/fabrication or induction of illness in a child by a carer;

- foetal abuse, for example, through maternal abuse of alcohol or drugs;

- domestic abuse (primarily of mothers) which causes physical or emotional abuse of children;

- children affected by parental drug abuse;

- racial abuse;

- female genital mutilation (circumcision);

- forced marriage; and

- children who need protecting from harming themselves, through self inflicted injuries or reckless behaviour.

1.5

It has become clear over the last twenty years that the agencies and individuals with responsibility for children do not always protect them. We are now more aware of institutional abuse, for example, physical, emotional or sexual abuse in care homes or schools. More recently 'system abuse' has been identified where the child protection or criminal justice systems or practices, in themselves, are experienced by children as being abusive. For example, children may experience medical examinations as abusive or they may be distressed by having to attend court.

1.6

Children and young people may not always define child abuse and neglect in terms used by official agencies. They tend to view child abuse primarily in terms of physical abuse and sexual abuse and are less likely to talk about physical neglect or emotional abuse. Research has shown that some children and young people experiencing abuse may not define it as such because they have learned to regard it as normal or deserved. Peer abuse has been identified as a major worry for children and young people, but bullying is not normally defined as child abuse by professionals.

What is child protection?

1.7

For many people the term child protection relates to the activities of agencies such as the police and social work services in their protection of individual children. Our study of public views suggests that this is the most common understanding. For others, it encompasses a wider range of activities such as making roads safer for children to cross, or educating children about drugs and other harmful substances. In this review we have examined closely those agencies involved in protecting individual children, but we also take a broader approach to understanding how children might be protected and consider preventative measures.

What is the extent of child abuse and neglect?[1]

1.8

Whilst it is impossible to measure the real extent of child abuse and neglect the following figures provide an important background:

- 670 children under 15 died during 2001, the majority of these deaths were health related, but 19 related to road accidents, eight to fires, two to suicides and 32 to Sudden Infant Death Syndrome.

- There were 10 child homicide victims in 2000.

- The number of persons proceeded against where the main offence was child abuse was 436 in 2000 (231 for sexual offences; 205 for non-sexual offences).

- 6,600 children were referred to social work departments in relation to child protection issues in 2000-2001.

- There were 2,000 children on the child protection register as at 31 March 2001.

- In 2000-2001, 22,436 children and young people were referred to the Reporter on non-offence grounds.

- ChildLine Scotland received 4,330 calls about abuse from new callers in 2000-2001.

[1] The statistics and information presented in this chapter come from the following sources: General Register Office Scotland; Scottish Executive; Scottish Children's Reporter Administration; ChildLine Scotland; Information and Statistics Division Scotland; Department for Work and Pensions; Department of Health; Scottish Women's Aid; Centre for Drug Misuse Research, University of Glasgow.

1.9

These figures do not, however, reflect the true level of child abuse and neglect for the following reasons:

- Much abuse and neglect does not come to the attention of official agencies because children do not tell anyone they are being abused. Research studies, which ask people whether they experienced abuse or neglect in their childhood, result in far higher numbers of people reporting that they have experienced abuse.

- Deaths from child abuse are very difficult to quantify and research suggests that some child abuse and neglect deaths may be miscoded as deaths due to natural causes or accidents.

- The victim's age is not recorded by the police for some sexual crimes such as rape and for most offences involving physical violence.

- ChildLine are able to answer less than half (48%) of the calls made to them.

1.10

Scottish child protection statistics do not include information about ethnic background, disability or other factors, which might help service planning.

1.11

National figures suggest that a parent is the abuser in over three-quarters of reported child abuse and neglect cases. In calls to ChildLine Scotland in 2000-2001, parents were generally cited as the abusers in cases of physical abuse and neglect, but in fewer than 40% of cases in relation to sexual and emotional abuse. In some cases, children and young people were being sexually and seriously physically abused by their peers.

The changing social context

1.12

Recent Scottish Executive reports, including *For Scotland's Children* and *Getting Our Priorities Right* have shown that, of the one million children in Scotland, many are living in poverty or are suffering as a result of family breakdown, parental drug and alcohol misuse and domestic abuse.

1.13

Deprivation undoubtedly increases the risk of family problems, and levels of child poverty in Scotland are high. Levels of deprivation are particularly high in Glasgow where 42% of children are entitled to free school meals and 42% of children under 16 live in families dependent on income support. Scotland's poorest children are four times more likely to be killed in a road accident than the wealthiest and nine times more likely to die in a fire in the home. Links between deprivation and child abuse and neglect are, however, contentious. For example, national Scottish statistics do not show clear linkages between levels of deprivation and the percentage of children on child protection registers or the percentage of child protection referrals. Other research has demonstrated, however, that there is a connection, particularly in relation to neglect. National statistics do suggest a link between levels of deprivation in an area and the percentage of children who are looked after.

1.14

Family structures have changed considerably over the past century. Now, in any one year approximately 8,000 children live in families where their parents are divorcing and many more are likely to experience the separation of their unmarried parents. One in five households are headed by a lone parent and more than 280,000 children live in lone parent households. It is likely that children's experiences of family life have been affected by these changes in family structures. We know, for example, that the divorce or separation of parents and disputes over contact can be very stressful for children and this is borne out by the case audit findings.

1.15

Over the past few decades there has been a decrease in the proportion of children and young people living in residential accommodation and an increase in the proportion of those living in foster care. Although research has shown that outcomes may be better in foster care, foster places are not always available.

1.16

The level of teenage pregnancies has been highlighted as a concern. Though falling, the rate of teenage conception in Scotland remains the highest in Europe and the rate in the most deprived area of Scotland is over six times higher than in the least deprived areas. Young parenthood presents its own difficulties and these are compounded by poverty.

Drug and alcohol misuse

1.17

Many children are affected by parental drug and alcohol misuse in Scotland:

- New research suggests there may be between 40,594 and 58,916 children with a drug-using parent in Scotland.

- Between 9,391 and 19,553 children appear to be living with a drug-using parent.

- The number of babies born to drug-misusing mothers has almost doubled, rising from 9.3 hospital discharges per 1,000 maternity cases in 1996-1997 to 17.7 in 1999-2000.

Domestic abuse

1.18

A significant number of children are witnessing or experiencing violence. It has been estimated that around 100,000 children in Scotland live with domestic abuse and that in 90% of incidents, children are in the same or next room. In addition to the emotional impact of living in an atmosphere of violence, there is also evidence to suggest that men who abuse their partners may also abuse their children, or force them to participate in the abuse of their mothers. Children often try to protect their mothers from physical assaults, and may be injured themselves as a result. Children living with domestic abuse may suffer from stress-related illnesses and conditions and experience feelings of guilt, shame, anger, fear and helplessness.

Signposts to success

1.19

Whilst, for some children, the outlook is bleak, there have been a number of improvements in Scotland that clearly show change is possible and children's lives can be improved:

- The death rate of children under 1 year of age has reduced from 8.6 in 1989 to 4.9 in 1999 per 1,000 population.

- The incidence of Sudden Infant Death Syndrome (SIDS) fell from 128 in 1990 to 33 in 2000 due mainly to a more stringent diagnosis of SIDS and the 'Back to sleep' campaign which advised parents to lay children on their backs.

- Fewer children are living in low income households (the proportion of children who were living in households below poverty thresholds[2] fell from 34% in 1996-1997 to 25% in 1999-2000 in real terms).

- The number of women smoking at the start of pregnancy has reduced from 28% in 1993 to 25% in 2000.

- Children are now much less likely to be routinely hit by their parents as a form of discipline than they were a generation ago.

- The greater recognition of children's rights in Scottish society.

Appendix C outlines the legal framework in relation to child protection in Scotland. It also describes the way in which agencies respond to allegations of abuse and neglect.

[2] Sixty per cent of the median income thresholds in Scotland (after housing costs have been accounted for).

"It's everyone's job to make sure I'm alright."

The Children in the case audit sample

The children

The nature of abuse

What were the reasons for abuse?

Key messages

2.1

The audit methodology identified a broad sample of children who were experiencing a wide range of abuse and neglect.

The Children

2.2

The sample consisted of 100 girls and 88 boys ranging in age from 1 month to 17 years.[3] The age and gender of the sample is shown below.

Figure 2: The age and gender of the sample

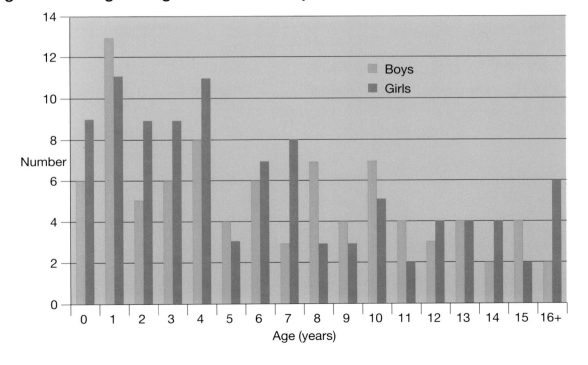

---

[3] In general, child protection procedures apply to children of 16 years and under. However, in the case of children with disabilities and looked after children they are extended to include 17 and 18 year olds.

2.3

From the information provided by the various agencies, the majority of children were identified as white, although there were nine mixed race children, two Asian/Pakistani and one Black/African. There were two children of Iranian asylum seekers. We asked agencies to provide information according to the OPCS classification.[4] Many did not or were unable to provide this information and it appears that information about ethnicity and race is not routinely collected by all the agencies we inspected.

Figure 3: The ethnic origin of the sample

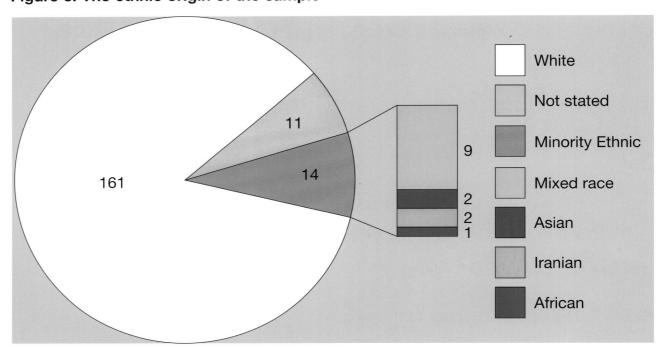

2.4

Twenty-two children were noted, by practitioners, to have emotional and behavioural difficulties and 18 to have some form of special needs. The fact that special needs were not noted did not necessarily mean that children did not have them.

2.5

Wider definitions of child abuse, for example runaway youth, underage sexual activity, child prostitution or forced marriages did not appear as the initial reason for referral or concern. Although agencies indicate that these are child protection issues, they did not appear in sufficient numbers to have formed part of the sample.

2.6

The majority of cases involved one child or a sibling group and one parent or parents. There were no cases in the sample of institutional abuse, internet abuse or children where it was alleged that there were a number of abusers.

[4] The Office of Population, Censuses and Surveys' classification system.

Table 1: Comparison of sample with national statistics

Primary Abuse Category	Number	(%)	National % in 2000
Physical Neglect	31	(39.7)	33.8
Physical Injury	24	(30.8)	37.7
Sexual Abuse	11	(14.1)	15.1
Emotional Abuse	10	(12.8)	12.4
Failure to Thrive	2	(2.6)	1.0 (categorised as 'other')

2.7

Half the children (95 of the 188) were on the child protection register. The main reason for registration was provided in 78 cases; a secondary reason was also given in 24 cases. Compared with the Scottish figures for 2000, the case audit sample had more children registered for physical neglect and fewer for physical injury.

2.8

The reasons for registration are not, however, a good indication of the nature of abuse most of the children experienced because:

- many children experienced more than one form of abuse;

- knowledge about other forms of abuse sometimes emerged after registration; and

- some forms of abuse were more easily evidenced than others and so were noted for registration purposes.

The nature of abuse

Neglect

2.9

Agencies noted neglect in 53 cases. There were a further 32 cases where parental skills or life style (with a high risk of neglect) were noted as major concerns. Overall, we estimated that 85 children (between a third and a half of the sample) were experiencing neglect.

2.10

There were some very serious cases of neglect. Sometimes the full extent of abuse and neglect became apparent only after a child was removed from home. In addition to the more evident signs of neglect children also suffered from lack of adequate sleep, absence of an effective structure to their lives and poor self-esteem. Very young children did not meet their developmental milestones as a result of inadequate food and stimulation.

> The Smith children were often late for school, arriving tired, grubby with shoes and outerwear unsuitable for wet and cold weather, for example, toeless sandals on a frosty morning. They did not do homework, had poor dental hygiene and missed medical appointments. Sarah's hearing in one ear was impaired because of untreated ear infections. The children were often left unsupervised in the care of their older sister. They experienced a series of untreated accidents and injuries at home, including burns, cuts and bruises.
>
> Food rubbish and general debris strewn about the floor ... dirty clothing lying in piles ... broken window ... very, very cold, thin duvet on cot in corner of the room ... smelled of urine, two wet patches on floor where the child is clearly urinating ... the flat is run down and has no source of central heating ... extremely cold and damp ... no appropriate cooking facilities or anywhere suitable to eat ... house was decrepit and inappropriate for three young children.
>
> Rosie (6) and Sophie (7) came to a foster carer very dirty, smelly, with head lice and long, dirty fingernails. All their clothes had to be thrown away. They were clingy, demanding and wet themselves or urinated in their bedroom. One of the children would get up in the night to take food from the fridge.

Physical injury

2.11

In 43 cases there were concerns about actual or risk of physical injury. Babies were particularly vulnerable to physical abuse. Injuries also occurred as parents struggled to cope with children's behavioural problems. Some children experienced physical violence from peers or from siblings.

> Five-month-old Tara was slapped and bruised by her mother.
>
> Three-month-old Joe was shaken by his father to the extent that he was seriously ill.
>
> Martin was scratched and bitten by his mother. He showed very aggressive behaviour towards other children.
>
> Fourteen-year-old Stuart had subjected his younger sister to at least one serious assault. His sister and his mother were frightened of him.

Sexual abuse

2.12

Thirteen children were registered because of sexual abuse. For many others sexual abuse was an unsubstantiated concern. Abuse included exposure to pornographic material, sexual innuendo, inappropriate touching, oral sexual activities and penetration. Almost all sexual abuse was committed by men, usually fathers, maternal partners, grandfathers or neighbours, but an aunt, stepsister, half-sister and siblings were also implicated as perpetrators. Some children were subjected to unwanted sexual behaviour from other children. Sometimes this could be explained as sexual exploration, but on occasion it was more explicit.

Paul and Michelle were sexually abused over a number of years by their maternal grandfather. He had also sexually abused their mother when she was a child.

Eight-year-old John was thrown to the ground in the playground by a peer and sexually assaulted.

Nine-year-old David subjected his sister to an invasive sexual assault. He had had serious behavioural problems for years.

Emotional abuse

2.13

Only 19 (10%) of the 188 children were registered on the grounds of emotional abuse. All forms of abuse and neglect have an emotional impact upon children, however, and the number of children we encountered who were subjected to direct emotional abuse exceeded the numbers who were formally registered under this category.

2.14

In many but not all instances, children's emotional difficulties were related to other forms of child abuse and parental substance abuse. Some children were not deliberately emotionally abused by their parents, but in putting their own needs first, parents caused emotional difficulties for their children. The children's emotional problems often related to the inability of the adults in their lives to provide a firm and loving structure for them.

Anthony was constantly subjected to racial abuse by his white father, as was his black mother.

'I have never, in a career of over 20 years, encountered such a case. Mother showed no love or concern for the child, where he had unconditional love for his mum' (Primary headteacher).

Baby Sean, a very unhappy, poorly baby, was, according to his mother, a 'grumpy little shit' shortly before his death.

The children were allowed to play in their bedrooms but nowhere else in the house. Their stepfather threatened to kill them and their pets and one weekend made a bonfire of all their toys.

Impact of problem drug or alcohol misuse or domestic abuse

2.15

Seventy-six children were living with parental substance misuse. Where parents had serious addiction problems, children were at risk when their parents were affected by drugs. Health visitors or social workers found parents incapable in the house when they visited and young children at risk from fires or other household appliances. Some parents tried to protect their children from knowledge of their drug use and from possible harm by locking them in their bedrooms for long periods of the day or night. This solution created its own abusive problems, not least children urinating and soiling in their bedrooms.

2.16

As a result of their parents' alcohol or drug misuse school-age children often adopted the role and burdens of caring both for the adults in their lives and for younger siblings.

Baby Adele was carried along the harbour wall by her father who was under the influence of drugs. Neighbours thought this action carried the risk of dropping her into the water.

Amy was recorded as collecting silver paper in the nursery playground because 'my mummy needs it'. (Silver paper is used by drug addicts when preparing or using drugs such as heroin.)

2.17

Domestic abuse featured in at least 56 cases. In some cases it formed the main concern and was an enduring feature of the child's life – one man who was violent to his wife had also physically assaulted three of his children; another man threw a child across the room during an attempt to murder the mother. In other cases domestic abuse was a background feature, referred to in files, reports and interviews as one of a range of stresses in the family likely to impact upon the children.

> Rachel's drug-using mother suffered a violent attack from her ex-partner and her brother Craig was moved to another home. Rachel was 'asking if it was her fault that she did not see her brother regularly'. She had no confidence that her interests came first. The primary school described her as a 'treasure' but expressed concerns over her lost childhood and the effects of being a carer.

Self-harm

2.18

In a small number of cases, the main risk to the children and young people derived from their own uninhibited or risky behaviours:

- aggression and violence;

- lack of a sense of danger;

- self-harming; and

- inappropriate sexual activity.

In some instances these behaviours were linked to very low self-esteem and possible previous experiences of abuse. In other cases conditions such as ADHD (attention deficit hyperactivity disorder) provided the trigger. Some abused children's behaviour was so harmful to other children, adults or property that distinguishing between the risks they faced and the risks they posed was not possible. It seemed that, the older a child was, the more likely they were to be perceived as an 'offender'. Sometimes this was the only route through which they might receive help, as in the case of a 15-year-old boy referred to the Reporter on offence grounds, but who had been identified as needing help from age 2.

> Eight-year-old Callum had experienced emotional abuse all his life as a result of his mother's long history of drinking and attempted suicides. His older brother and sister had also experienced sexual and physical abuse by their mother's former partner. Callum had witnessed his mother and other members of his family attempting suicide. He showed seriously aggressive behaviour towards other children in school and, on one occasion, attempted to kill himself. He had cut himself with a knife, had viciously attacked the family pets, thrown bricks at cars and at a baby in a pram.

What were the reasons for abuse?

2.19

There were a number of identifiable causes of abuse:

- parents who lacked adequate parenting skills, often as a result of weaknesses in their own upbringing – in 14 cases parents were recorded as having experienced abuse or neglect in their childhood; a further 21 mothers and two fathers had been in care;

- parents with addictions to alcohol or drugs who consistently or at times of pressure gave greater priority to their addiction needs than to their children's welfare (76);

- parents who lacked effective budgeting and prioritising skills (15);

- physically- or sexually-abusing adults within the family or extended family (16);

- parents with mental health problems (48);

- unstable family groupings which resulted in children being exposed to changing and often unsuitable parental role models; and

- bitter marriage or relationship break-ups where children's welfare became a source of conflict for parents.

2.20

More mothers than fathers were identified as having problems but more children were brought up by lone mothers and agencies focused more on mothers' parenting skills than they did on fathers. In one case a mother, rather than both parents, was prosecuted for neglect.

Key messages

- Many children experience very serious levels of hurt and harm and are forced to live in miserable and unhappy situations.

- Many children are subject to more than one type of abuse or neglect; the reasons for registration are not a good indication of the nature of the abuse most children experience.

- It is clear that parents' serious personal and social problems are the cause of much harm to their children.

Chapter 2: The children in the case audit sample

"It's everyone's job to make sure I'm alright."

The case audit: Protecting children

3.1

The previous chapter clearly sets out the extent of the challenge for practitioners working to protect children and to improve their lives. Few of the children were known to only one agency and we were, therefore, able to consider individual and multi-agency responses to these complex situations.

Raising concerns about a child

3.2

In very few of the 188 cases were concerns about a child's welfare minimal, or the result of a 'one-off' or trivial incident. Even those cases (34) on the health visitor's cause for concern list were generally considered to be 'in need' and some were on the Child Protection Register.

3.3

Most of the children had been known to agencies as in need of assistance for a considerable time or had been previously referred for help on one or more occasion. The needs of the children were generally wider than just the need for protection due to a single incident. A 'referral' from one agency to another was sometimes an 'exchange of information', particularly when children were well known to both agencies. In these circumstances it was not always possible to clearly identify when the first significant concern about a child emerged.

3.4

As we will see in Chapter 6, very few children contact statutory agencies when they need help. Only seven of the 188 children in this sample self-referred to any agency:

- one girl reported sexual abuse to school;

- one girl reported physical abuse to school;

- four boys reported physical abuse to school but it was not clear whether the reporting was deliberate, or by way of explanation of other difficulties; and

- one girl phoned social work to say she did not want to go home as her parents had been drinking alcohol for a few days.

3.5

Most abuse was identified by third parties, normally health, education or the police, but others such as housing departments, Women's Aid or ChildLine also made referrals. Referrals rarely came from other agencies or organisations which are in regular contact with children or adults who might harm them. There were no referrals, for example, from youth clubs/associations, sports or leisure clubs, churches, drug misuse agencies or organisations working with parents. In many cases relatives or neighbours contacted social work. A neighbour e-mailed a social work department about her concern over a child's failure to thrive and hostel residents raised concerns about the way other residents cared for their children. In one case a member of the public informed the police he had seen children playing in the bedroom of a single man. The man subsequently turned out to be a sex offender.

3.6

Where a member of the public or another agency raises a concern or where there are a number of smaller events or incidents that add up to a significant concern about a child's welfare, professionals consider whether they need to follow their local agency child protection guidance and formally refer the matter to social work services or the police. Child Protection guidance encourages internal agency discussion prior to referral. We found, however, that many health professionals did not know who their lead officer for reference was, and in schools, there were instances where the headteacher's absence from the premises resulted in delay in referring a child until his or her return.

3.7

Medical staff did not always make the necessary checks with other medical records to establish if an injury was part of a pattern which might indicate it was non-accidental.

3.8

Some health visitors and headteachers were reluctant to jeopardise relationships with a family by passing on their concerns to another agency. In a few cases this resulted in information not being shared promptly.

3.9

Some referrals were presented clearly and with good information but many referrals to social work were made by telephone and were not always followed up in writing as agency guidance generally stipulates.

3.10

Incidents coming to the attention of the police were referred promptly to both social work and the Reporter.

3.11

Some health visitors and education staff thought that their referrals to social work were not taken seriously enough. There were a number of reasons for this:

- a false expectation that an informal phone discussion would result in formal action being taken;

- single incidents were referred, when the real issue for the referrer was the cumulative effect over time;

- a lack of physical evidence of abuse; or

- a lack of detailed recording of concerns by the referrer.

> Good practice example:
>
> A nursery assistant was concerned about Jonathan's aggressive behaviour. The Officer in Charge asked her to observe and keep a record of his behaviour. The diary was maintained for a fortnight and showed a disturbing pattern of behaviour including sexual assaults on other children. The Officer in Charge spoke with social work services and provided them with a copy of the diary. On receipt of the information social work was able to begin an investigation with clear unequivocal information.

3.12

There was a general perception by all agencies that it was social work's responsibility to take the lead in protecting children. There were few exceptions to this and even where there were it was rarely on the first occasion that another agency took independent action.

3.13

Most education authorities had procedures whereby all formal referrals to social work were automatically copied to the Reporter. In most areas the police had a policy of routinely referring to both social work and the Reporter every child present in the house during a domestic abuse incident. We were told by other agencies, particularly Reporters, that this resulted in a huge increase in referrals, mostly unaccompanied by evidence of need or risk.

3.14

Good practice in the recognition and referral of abuse was found when:

- all professionals working with children could identify signs of abuse and neglect and knew how to respond;

- referring agencies produced a written referal detailing the circumstances, behavours or incidents of concern; and

- social work and the police responded promptly to concerns.

Initial enquiry and investigation

3.15

When social work or the police receive a referral they must consider:

- the needs of the child;

- whether a referral should be made to the Reporter;

- if particular child protection measures should be taken; and

- if there should be a criminal investigation or prosecution.

3.16

In order to make decisions about how to proceed, further initial enquiries may be necessary. In some cases enquiries were not sufficiently extensive. In many interviews we were told that agency records and the Child Protection Register were consulted at the start of each investigation or enquiry, yet this was often not recorded on the files. We also found one case where a man's criminal convictions were not checked by police until after a case conference. Medical practitioners did not always seek the full medical history of or background information about children who presented with an injury. A number of police investigations did not involve extensive interviewing of family members and rarely involved the interviewing of neighbours, even in those cases where neighbours had first raised the concern. The police did not always take DNA samples in serious cases from alleged abusers as guidance indicates.

> **Good practice examples:**
>
> James had sustained a broken leg, which the hospital considered to be non-accidental. Checks revealed previous concern and an acrimonious split between his parents. His aunt, both grandparents and parents were interviewed. Discrepancies in their accounts of events surrounding the discovery of the injury were fully investigated. Detailed statements were taken. Parental movements were traced through examining supermarket video records and checks with employers. A close examination of all the evidence collated confirmed that this was a non-accidental injury.
>
> A duty social worker who received a referral, later discovered that further checks had not been followed up. She had vague information that the father had other children elsewhere and tenaciously traced crucial background information from other social work departments in two other authorities.

3.17

We were also concerned about the narrow focus of enquiries. In most cases where there was a clearly identified incident of abuse, such as an assault or allegations of sexual abuse, the focus of the early work by police and social work was on establishing if the case was one of 'child protection' and if an offence had been committed. This required obtaining factual information or evidence about injuries and circumstances of the incident. This emphasis on evidence gathering sometimes led to the needs, particularly health needs, of the child, being a secondary consideration. Medicals were usually requested for 'evidential' rather than health or welfare purposes. Though there would have been good health reasons for doing so, police or social work did not initiate medical assessments or examinations as part of their enquiries where:

- a child had been hit so hard in the eye that his head 'ricocheted back';
- a child, who was exhibiting sexualised behaviour complained of a 'sore bum' for nine months;
- there were regular reports of hungry children; and
- children were not receiving health care, including attention to hearing, sight and dental problems.

> A referral was made to social work regarding a possible cigarette burn to Ryan. Social work investigated the incident. The police were not involved although it was possible that the injuries had been deliberately inflicted. There was no forensic medical examination and there were no enquiries with the boy's primary school even though the school had regularly logged detailed concerns regarding injury and emotional disturbance with social work over the previous three months.
>
> Paul was born withdrawing from drugs and his mother's partner was violent to her. A year after his birth he was found to have extensive bruising and was also failing to thrive. His mother was also bruised. There was no investigation of who might be responsible for the injuries. Medical records were illegible, poorly kept and some parts were missing. There was no assessment of Paul's needs or of his mother's ability to meet them. Paul remained at risk of abuse.

3.18

In only one area was there a procedure for routine discussions with education during enquiries. In some areas routine 'initial referral discussions' held jointly with health, the police and social work took place at an early stage of investigations or enquiries but this was not the norm across the country. Where we saw examples of good multi-agency approaches they had a positive impact on planning future work.

3.19

Where medical opinion had been sought, social work and the police were highly dependent upon that opinion as to the cause of injuries or symptoms. In some of these cases, an ambivalent medical opinion was cited by police and social work as preventing them from taking action to protect the child.

> 'It was impossible to determine the cause of the lesions nor could it be stated as to whether they were accidental or non-accidental in nature.' (Knuckle injuries to 1-month-old Rachel who was subsequently found with similar injuries to the other hand a week later, and was taken into care shortly after.)

3.20

In three cases, where there were serious concerns about the current welfare of children in the family, previous children of one of the parents had died. In each case the medical opinion had been that there was no evidence to indicate that the deaths were suspicious. In one case (which we could not consider in detail because proceedings were ongoing) a previous child of the father had died. In another case the father of a child who died had had two previous children, by different women, who had also died. The cause of both deaths had been recorded as Sudden Infant Death Syndrome. In the third case a child's sibling had died and the death was recorded as SIDS. Previous deaths of children in a family in combination with current concerns about children's welfare heightened concern. But professionals, particularly social work, felt unable to take protective action as a diagnosis of SIDs implied that no concerns were evident in previous care. Many professionals thought that more in-depth enquiries into the circumstances of some children's deaths may reveal parenting practices that should inform future child care decisions.

3.21

Whilst joint planning of investigations or enquiries was a feature of good practice, we did not find that Joint Police/Social Work Units for child protection necessarily resulted in significantly better handling of cases.

3.22

Occasionally, the effectiveness of an investigation was hampered by lack of equipment, or lack of practitioners experienced in the use of specialist equipment. In some cases, children had to be driven considerable distances for a medical examination. In another case a child's interview was not properly recorded due to broken equipment.

3.23

In a few cases, there were significant delays in conducting investigations when children moved across police division boundaries or across local authority boundaries. In such cases the child's needs were lost sight of in discussions over responsibilities.

3.24

In almost all the cases reviewed, the impact of the investigation on the child was at the forefront of professionals' thinking. Investigations were conducted sensitively and at the pace of the child. If necessary, interviews were suspended if a child became upset. Only rarely were children required to return for further interviews. Agencies ensured that, where possible, duplication was minimised. We concluded that the experience for most of the children interviewed had been as sensitively handled as possible given the nature of the complaints.

> **Good practice example:**
>
> A police officer enabled a child to familiarise herself with the interview room and police officer's role through using her police hat, belt and epaulettes as 'playthings'.

3.25

There were particular problems if the children had significant learning and/or communication difficulties. One girl's complaint to the police was not proceeded with on the basis of her potential 'unreliability' as a witness. In these cases, specialist resources could have been employed to enable children to express themselves better, to gather additional evidence or to provide an expert assessment of evidence reliability, but we did not see any examples of this.

3.26

Effective investigations and enquiries were characterised by:

- full gathering of information from all relevant sources;

- police investigating thoroughly, for example, taking DNA samples and searching for evidence to corroborate the accounts of children, parents and suspects;

- doctors seeking full medical information when examining the presenting injury, particularly previous accident and emergency visits, and taking account of social history from all sources in drawing conclusions;

- social workers seeking and taking account of the information held by other agencies;

- sensitive interviewing of children and attention to their needs; and

- using medical examinations to identify health care needs – not just evidence gathering.

Recording of investigations

3.27

Many investigations were poorly recorded across professions. Hospital accident and emergency records described injuries, but not the circumstances of their occurrence, and incidents tended to be considered in isolation. Social work files contained details of the processes undertaken, but often did not contain investigation details or copies of witness statements. Most agency records summarised concerns about children rather than providing the detail needed for any future reopening of the case or future investigations. Some Reporters' files, in accordance with agency policy, were 'weeded' to the point that essential information was missing when a new concern arose. Such weaknesses made it difficult for practitioners to recognise patterns of incidents.

> A house was recorded in the file as 'falling below acceptable standards' but workers described it to the review team as 'absolutely filthy' and 'all the kitchen surfaces were covered with dirty plates and old food'.

Initial assessments

3.28

From the initial identification of a child protection concern, professionals working with children had to make assessments about risks and needs. There were some positive examples of good initial assessments. Generally police and social work had access to information to help them make an initial assessment. Medical practitioners, however, particularly those in adult accident and emergency units, frequently had insufficient information on which to make a sound initial assessment, and were unaware of other relevant records. They sometimes only had access to their unit's records when key medical information concerning the child was contained in separate case notes covering child protection, child development, and mental health. In one area, up to 11 separate medical records were kept on children.

3.29

There were also problems when children, for one reason or another, had moved between authorities, with a consequent dispersal of records. In one instance an emotionally damaged boy had attended 12 schools in three authorities and two countries over six years. It was difficult to piece together an appropriately detailed picture of him and his history.

> A joint paediatric-forensic medical was performed, but no information on Melissa was available in the community child health records. She was later subjected to a further genital examination by another consultant paediatrician, at her GP's request.
>
> Fifteen-year-old Daniel attended the local children's hospital on multiple occasions for minor injuries. Each injury had been treated in isolation. Hospital staff did not check other health records and so did not link his injuries to his behavioural problems noted elsewhere. An opportunity was missed to address the cause of the injuries.

Full assessments

3.30

In many cases concerns about children were ongoing and each incident or event of concern in a child's life was one of many factors to be considered as part of an assessment.

3.31

Assessments of what immediate action needed to be taken were generally sound but longer-term assessment of the risks to children was poor. Some children were subject to a number of assessments since different disciplines, Hearings and meetings require different assessments of different aspects of children's lives. Most of the children in the sample were assessed prior to case conferences and Hearings and a number had other assessments for specialist services.

> Joanna had a total of six assessments – child protection, Hearing, school behavioural support, as a 'looked after' child, speech therapy and a specialist project for children with behavioural problems.

3.32

In complex cases, more comprehensive assessments were needed. In these cases, assessments usually required the collaboration of a number of professionals. This was not always forthcoming – an accident and emergency consultant refused to discuss with a child's social worker an incident of abuse requiring hospital treatment. Some schools did not keep social work informed of serious incidents involving children at risk – one boy's social worker only heard of an assault when he was asked to prepare a report for the Children's Hearing.

3.33

In the majority of cases, social work was the primary agency for assessing the needs of children at risk. In conducting assessments, social workers often had a wealth of relevant information but it was not always readily accessible. The case audit team found key information, sometimes going back 10 or 20 years, that was 'buried' in the files and had not been included in the assessment: in one case a man convicted of sexual offences against children in the 1960s was now caring for his grandchildren; in another a father of five children, about whom there were concerns about possible sexual abuse, had convictions for sex offences dating back to his youth. In many other cases we saw patterns of behaviour, usually related to poor parenting, being repeated with later children, sometimes a decade apart. Again the information was there but not readily accessible.

3.34

There were few examples of good, comprehensive written assessments. Weaknesses included:

- failure to consider the chronology and pattern of previous events;

- insufficient use of inter-agency information, especially health and education;

- insufficient attention to the role of at least one key person in the child's life – most commonly the mother's partner or ex-partner;

- lack of focus on the child – for example, the assessment of a child of drug-using parents focused on the parents' problems rather than the child's needs; and

- social workers not applying for an Assessment Order in the face of parents' non-co-operation.

'... we have to give every chance of making it work, do the utmost to see if this is the one she's going to make it with'. (A social worker discussing a case where a child had died whose siblings had all been taken into care in the past because of neglect.)

3.35

Much information provided had to be treated with caution. Grandparents, understandably, often offered over-optimistic views regarding family progress. Professionals, such as drug misuse workers reported on clients' progress and stability. Whilst that progress might be viewed as adequate for adults, in some cases it was not sufficient for adults who were also parents.

> Seven-year-old Melanie had suffered various forms of parental abuse and neglect from birth. Her siblings had previously been removed from their mother's care following identical allegations. Earlier allegations about Melanie were not properly investigated and she was 6 before there was a full investigation and action taken. By then she had a number of problems – educational, social, sexual and behavioural. She was now secure with foster carers but there were indications that they might not be able to cope with her long term.
>
> Michael lived with his mother who had drug and alcohol problems. Her partner was violent and it was alleged that he had hit the children. The children were said to be 'terrified' of their stepfather and neglected by their mother. Mother was well supported with a range of social worker services and addiction services were also providing support. The children benefited from nursery placements, respite care and home support. Every effort was made to ensure that their immediate needs were met and the children spent as little time at home as possible. No action was taken to remove the violent partner from the home or to remove the children, however. Services were provided without an assessment of the children's longer-term needs – whether their mother would ever be able to meet them or if more assertive action in relation to her partner was needed.

3.36

In a number of cases, staffing changes resulted in long, drawn-out and inconclusive assessments.

3.37

Frequently there were inadequate assessments of the parents' ability to make use of the support on offer and to change quickly and sufficiently enough to offer their children an acceptable level of care. This was particularly an issue in relation to young children whose parents had already had older children taken into care. In these cases there was rarely a full assessment of:

- the parents' capacity to care and protect;

- the extent to which their circumstances or skills had improved for the better since the birth of previous children; and

- the steps the parents had taken to ensure a repetition might be avoided in the future.

3.38

In a number of cases the *risks* were clear, but social workers could not remove children without clear *evidence* of current abuse.

3.39

In some cases, services such as home support, nursery or day care were provided without a full assessment of need – perhaps on the recommendation of a health visitor or school. In other cases, support was provided as a response to evident immediate need. In these cases support staff were able to monitor the child or family's progress but were not in a position to take the longer-term overview that was so badly needed.

3.40

It was often difficult to establish exactly what assessment had been undertaken, due to the absence of clear, well-focused records. Assessments, but not necessarily full assessments, appeared in a variety of reports and, occasionally, assessments formed a part of the case record.

> Good practice example:
>
> Matt (12) was physically assaulted by his mother and a referral to social work was made through ChildLine who arranged for the police to meet him at a phonebox. The incident was investigated, a risk assessment undertaken by social work and Matt was placed on the register with a view to a three-month assessment. Help to both Matt and his mother was provided by social work from the outset. Both engaged in individual work – mother on anger management and Matt on working with authority, particularly teachers. There was also joint work on their relationship. The case was deregistered after the three-month assessment period.

3.41

In those cases where we identified practice as being very good, clear planning to meet the child's short- and long-term needs was reflected in good written assessment records characterised by:

- well-structured assessment frameworks;

- clear details of the behaviour(s) or incident(s) of concern;

- a focus on the child's needs;

- a focus on the parent's ability to meet them; and

- action needed to reduce risk both in the short and long-term and to meet the wider needs of the child.

3.42

Additionally good assessment records clearly separated fact from opinion and were based on the most up-to-date knowledge about child abuse and neglect and best practice.

Case conferences and reviews

3.43

Once investigations or enquiries had been conducted and initial or full assessments completed, social work, sometimes in conjunction with other agencies, decided whether or not to hold a case conference. Social work based this decision on the level of risk faced by the child and whether the best way of protecting the child and addressing his/her needs was through multi-agency action. If this was the case they sought to place the child's name on the Child Protection Register, and to involve other agencies. A referral to the Reporter would also be considered if this had not happened already. Other agencies, however, saw placement on the register less in terms of the need for multi-agency work and more as a means of guaranteeing resources for the child, so there were often clear differences of opinion about the appropriateness of registration. Child protection registers were originally created to keep track of families moving from one area to another and this function seems to have been lost sight of.

3.44

The quality of case conferences, as evidenced by the minutes and plans deriving from them, was variable, as was attendance by agencies other than social work. Good structures for inter-agency case conferences and reviews proved very effective mechanisms for ensuring issues were identified, needs assessed and progress maintained. Where structures were less clear, the case audit found a number of recurring problems:

- lack of involvement of key personnel, including, on occasions, key members of the child's family;

- failure over a significant period of time to clearly assess needs;

- a lack of clarity as to whether the child's or the parents' needs took priority;

- lack of a clear plan of action;

- confusion between activity and progress; and

- uncertainty over the means of decision making which could give rise to serious resentment.

3.45

Good inter-agency attendance and co-operation at conferences helped ensure a full consideration of the needs of both children and parents and of the range of support options available. Relevant agencies did not always attend. Schools did not generally attend case conferences in school holidays and GPs rarely attended and were reluctant to share information. The amount of information drugs or mental health workers felt able to share varied and was sometimes dependent on agreements with patients. In one case a health visitor was not invited although a previous sibling had died from Sudden Infant Death Syndrome. In some areas, social work 'reviewing officers' chaired all case conferences and were able to retain an overview of the risks and needs of children.

> **Good practice example:**
>
> A mental health nurse (drug misuse) provided good information to case conferences. Her clients signed a mandate for her to share information with doctors and criminal justice and children's social workers where necessary. She advised others when the drug misuse increased or when it became chaotic providing a realistic assessment of progress. She promptly referred any concerns about children's welfare.

3.46

Joint planning could be particularly useful in maintaining current support mechanisms, for example, within the extended family, or through the school, even where a decision was made to move a child from the immediate family.

3.47

There were difficulties when agencies with crucial information about children were in another area or, in some instances, different countries. We found that, generally, case conferences did not fully involve out of area agencies, and often were content to receive their views as reported by another contributor. In two cases foster carers provided comments on how children were doing in new schools in a new local authority area.

3.48

In some areas, voluntary and private organisations were not included in case conferences. In one instance this resulted in important information held by a private nursery being overlooked.

3.49

At case conferences, the views of the children themselves were often not fully considered, or heard only as presented through third parties because:

- children refused to become involved;

- they were reluctant to express views critical of their parents in their presence;

- they felt overwhelmed by the setting;

- children under secondary age were regularly excluded from case conferences, even where it was clear that they could give an informed view; or

- where several children of the same family were involved, the needs of different children were not considered separately, for example, in one family of three children, the oldest boy regarded any placement other than with his mother as an improvement, while his youngest sister pined to return home.

3.50

In one or two areas children were encouraged to write their views prior to the case conference or Children's Hearing, and in almost all instances this opportunity was well used by the young people concerned. This can be a very effective way of helping children express their views, especially if they have difficulty in doing so in a meeting. Parents attending a Children's Hearing have a right to all the information that is being presented to the Hearing and this may include written statements about a child's wishes and views. Children, in preparing statements for the Hearing may not be aware of this. Evidence, from discussions with young people, indicates that the provision of such information may increase the risks to the child if parents are angry with the views expressed or wish to silence them. In the 'messages to young people' study there was one example of a girl, whose father had been convicted of assaulting her, who was advised that her statement would not be made available to either her mother or father. The statement was given to her father prior to the Hearing (but not to her mother). She was very distressed and stated she would not confide her views to anyone again in the future.

3.51

Some families felt overwhelmed by case conferences. Arrangements to provide families with support for conferences were variable, as was practice in ensuring that they fully understood the outcomes of the meeting. Sometimes key players, such as grandparents, were omitted from the discussion.

'The case conference was difficult, as I was fearful of losing my children. The case conference was explained, but I still found it difficult. Everyone was there and then I went in. I did not need to say very much, but if I'd had to, I'm not sure I would, I was so upset' (a mother).

'I went with mum and dad, but dad was not allowed in – it was too busy. I would have liked him there. The baby had to be watched, so dad did it, but she was sleeping. Social work could have watched her' (a mother).

3.52

Since case conferences are not statutory, any decisions they reach about agencies' intervention in families' lives, can only be implemented through one of three routes: voluntary co-operation, emergency powers or referral to the children's Reporter. Where parents refused to co-operate with the decisions of the case conference, agencies sometimes treated this as a cause for referral to the Reporter. Conversely, in some cases, parents were persuaded to agree to case conference decisions, or even to have their child looked after away from home on a voluntary basis, as a means of avoiding a referral to the Reporter.

3.53

Good practice in case conferencing was found when:

- case conferences were held timeously and the minutes of the conference were circulated promptly;

- all participants were clear about the purpose of the meeting, the process being followed, how decisions would be made and the conference recorded;

- all individuals and organisations with information to contribute attended and shared accurate information openly;

- both the discussion and the minutes distinguished between facts, inferences and assessments; and

- as far as possible children and parents were fully involved.

Referral to the Reporter

3.54

The purpose of the Children's Hearing system is to consider the need for compulsory orders in relation to children, taking account of the child's welfare throughout his or her childhood. In many cases of child abuse and neglect the nature of the abuse or the level of parental co-operation may suggest the need to consider having a legal order to underpin work with the child and family. In two-thirds of the cases in the audit sample, where a referral was made to social work or the police about abuse or neglect, a referral was made also to the Reporter, although not always for child protection reasons and not always in relation to the same incident. The referral may have been made at the same time as a referral was made about an incident to social work or the police. Alternatively it may have been made following another incident at another time or following initial enquiries or a case conference. In some cases referrals were made later if concerns remained or if families did not co-operate with agencies.

3.55

Children's Hearings also deal with referrals unrelated to abuse and neglect, for example, offending and truancy. The audit sample included two cases of young men (aged 13 and 15 years) about whom there had been previous concerns about abuse and neglect, who were now attending a Hearing on offence grounds.

3.56

The reasons for referral to the Reporter and the Reporter's grounds for registration could and often did, differ from those used for registering children as being in need of protection (see figure 4). Different sets of procedures, reports and information were required for different purposes and meetings (Hearings, case conferences, looked after children and other reviews.

Figure 4: Different reasons for intervention

Statutory Grounds of a Hearing's Jurisdiction

The child:

a) is beyond the control of any relevant person

b) is falling into bad associations or is exposed to moral danger

c) is likely to suffer unnecessarily, or be impaired seriously in his health or development, due to lack of parental care

d) is a child in respect of whom any of the offences mentioned in Schedule 1 to the Criminal Procedure (Scotland) Act 1995 (offences against children to which special provisions apply) has been committed

e) is, or is likely to become, a member of the same household as a child in respect of whom any of the offences referred to in paragraph (d) above has been committed

f) is, or is likely to become, a member of the same household as a person who has committed any of the offences referred to in paragraph (d) above

g) is, or is likely to become, a member of the same household as a person in respect of whom an offence under sections 1 to 3 of the Criminal Law (Consolidation) (Scotland) Act 1995 (incest and intercourse with a child by step-parent or person in position of trust) has been committed by a member of that household

h) has failed to attend school regularly without reasonable excuse

Children in Need
as defined in Children (Scotland) Act 1995

He or she is unlikely to achieve or maintain, or to have the opportunity of achieving or maintaining a reasonable standard of health or development unless the local authority provides services for him.

His or her health or development is unlikely to be significantly impaired, unless local authority services are so provided.

He or she is disabled.

He or she is affected adversely by the disability of any other person in his or her family.

Services may be provided with a view to safeguarding or promoting a child's welfare, for his or her family.

Services may be provided with a view to safeguarding or promoting a child's welfare, for any other member of his or her family.

Reasons for child protection

Child Protection Registration

When one or more of the following criteria for registration are met and the child's safety and welfare is considered to require an interagency child protection plan.

Physical injury

Sexual abuse

Non-organic failure to thrive

Emotional abuse

Physical neglect

3.57

Because the Children's Hearings have to decide on the need for compulsory measures of care, the bases for their decisions are necessarily defined in law. Some of the problems the different demands create might be eased by a more standard approach to assessments, and by making more straightforward use of case conference information in preparing Children's Hearing reports.

3.58

Reporters can request any information they think is relevant on a child from social work, education or any other agency. Local authority social workers are generally expected to provide all the necessary information on which the Reporter or a Hearing can base decisions. They did not always do so, for example, they did not always provide information about the health and achievement of, or developmental milestones of very young children. On only one occasion did a Reporter seek additional information from a health visitor. Both health and education practitioners made referrals to the Reporter about abuse and neglect, but most did not feel able to make an independent referral without the explicit support of social work.

3.59

Where the Reporter decided action was necessary and the child was young, or where the child or parents disputed or did not understand the grounds for referral, the case was referred to the sheriff court for a proof Hearing. This occurs in 80% of care and protection cases. In these circumstances, the less formal approach of the Hearing was replaced by a more adversarial one. We were told by both social services and Reporters that this sometimes made parental co-operation more difficult to achieve.

3.60

Reporters generally operated within the timescales given for processing paper work or arranging Hearings, but there were often significant delays in decision making, some of which were beyond their control. In some cases delays were caused by late presentation of reports by social workers (schools invariably produced reports on time). In one area, the Reporter had a list of outstanding reports, some of which were more than a year overdue. Reporters particularly commented on the burden of referrals in respect of domestic abuse cases, the majority of which they thought required 'No Further Action'.

Key messages

- Most cases of child abuse are referred to agencies by third parties, very few children or adults self-refer.

- Enquiries and investigations are not always sufficiently extensive and investigations are often poorly recorded.

- Assessment of what immediate action needs to be taken is generally sound but longer-term assessment of the risks to children is poor.

- Good inter-agency attendance and co-operation at case conferences helps ensure a full consideration of the needs of children and their parents.

- Children and their families experience a number of hearings, assessments and enquiries.

- There can be many delays in the Hearings system.

"It's everyone's job to make sure I'm alright."

The case audit: Meeting children's needs

4

4.1

The audit of practice showed that there was considerable work by professionals in respect of the children. The weight of concern was great and in many cases extensive energy and resources were deployed. In this chapter we discuss the kind of services offered and how effective they were in meeting children's needs. We also consider the extent to which children's lives were improved by agency intervention.

Immediate action

4.2

Some children needed immediate protection by removal from home. In the majority of such cases social workers and the police worked with parents to persuade them to agree to their children being moved elsewhere. There were occasions when parents would not co-operate with social work or other agencies, however, and risk remained. In these instances there was a need to consider taking out either a child protection order (CPO) to remove the child to a place of safety, or an exclusion order to remove the person who presented the risk, from the family home.

4.3

CPOs were rarely applied for. Social workers were reluctant to seek them unless they could demonstrate to a court that there was an immediate risk to the child. Some social workers were not confident about seeking one. A number of social workers expressed concern about appearing in court and being cross examined about their work. Other agencies often saw a CPO as a precaution to be taken in relation to something that might happen, for example, a parent deciding to remove a child from hospital against the advice of the doctors. Even where other agencies felt strongly that a CPO was necessary they did not use their own powers to seek one.

> Rachel was seen with bruising at hospital. Her mother was a drug user with a violent ex-partner. The paediatrician and police believed that a CPO was necessary but social work did not. The child remained at home and the paediatrician remained concerned. When asked whether she herself would consider seeking a CPO as the law provided, she stated that she thought it would not be granted without social work support.

4.4

Social workers generally held the view that there was little point in seeking exclusion orders as they placed the responsibility on the other adult in the household (usually a woman who had previously been unsuccessful in excluding the man) to keep the abuser out. We saw only one example of an exclusion order being used.

> Teenager Caroline was sexually abused by her mother's partner on whom there was an Exclusion Order. After an initial period of keeping him out of the house Caroline's mother gradually reverted to allowing him access, in part because he provided material and practical resources for the family. Caroline remained seriously at risk, but refused help from agencies stating that they had not previously protected her when they had an opportunity to do so. She had developed her own methods of protection which involved placing her friends at risk by having them stay with her and sleeping with a 'knife under her mattress'.

4.5

In a small number of cases children were at risk from males who were not living in the family home, but were living close by or were frequent visitors. The risks to children were sometimes very serious in such cases but the grounds for compulsory measures of supervision – that a child 'is likely to become a member of the same household' as an offender – could not be met. Reporters had difficulty in framing grounds in such cases and the Hearing system could not offer an effective way of protecting the child. Similarly when a child was showing sexualised behaviour, but no conclusive evidence was found that the child was being sexually abused, Reporters often struggled to frame grounds.

> Three-year-old Gemma referred frequently to her 'Uncle David' (a man who had served a four-year sentence for abusing children) when talking to social workers. Her mother denied that her brother had any contact with the family.

Longer-term action

4.6

Much of the abuse and neglect was the result of poor parenting skills. Once recognised, agencies normally responded with a range of compensatory measures to improve the day-to-day conditions for the children:

- increasing support in the home through home carers helping the children to rise and wash, getting them ready for school or nursery and preparing and providing meals;

- providing early or full-time nursery placements;

- schools, through breakfast clubs and school dinners, provided food and on occasions, supplementied clothing; and

- providing respite care.

4.7

The work by social workers and social work assistants, home care workers, teachers and classroom assistants often sustained children. Where there were problems of parental substance abuse, we found some evidence of high levels of home support stabilising situations. Home care workers also often provided a key liaison channel for health and education staff. Respite care allowed children to experience nurturing and develop new skills whilst retaining the family bond.

> **Good practice examples:**
>
> Poor feeding practice almost resulted in baby Laura starving to death. Both she and her mother (who had learning disabilities) were placed with a foster carer. This arrangement protected Laura whilst her mother was taught how to properly care for her. From the foster parent she learnt about the needs of young children and how to meet them, skills which were lacking in her own childhood.
>
> The parents of baby Alex were struggling to form an emotional bond with him. The health visitor taught them baby massage. Touching and relating to their baby helped them develop a relationship with him.

4.8

We saw a range of educative programmes for parents. Where support to improve parenting skills was offered, the contributions of family centres or nurseries were particularly impressive. In a few cases health visitors also played a significant part. Most services were either directed at women or both parents together. We came across only one example of special provision for men where a black Muslim health visitor voluntarily offered his services to fathers in the local mosque in his own time. The provision of such a service in this way suggests that provision for fathers is much needed but is not being developed by statutory agencies.

Home support

4.9

In some cases parents were greatly assisted in developing the ability to care effectively for their children.

4.10

Where intensive remedial work was provided solely in the home, we found little evidence of long-term success. In some cases it was not possible for home carers to engage in the educative role without first clearing and cleaning a space in which this might occur, for example, in food preparation or washing clothes. This resulted in many home carers 'doing' rather than educating and training as intended. Although home care support was often aimed at improving the cleanliness of both the home and that of the children, many children remained dirty, poorly clad and smelly. This left them open to bullying at school and within the community.

4.11

In several cases, children were living at home, but virtually all the day-to-day and occasional night care was provided by a range of support services rather than the parents. In reality the local authority was parenting the child.

4.12

In some instances children continued to suffer physical harm, in spite of considerable family support. Where additional support was provided through schools, there were examples of children's situations deteriorating over the school holidays. Most fundamentally, however, these arrangements did not address the lack of parental interest and care without which children's positive self-esteem cannot develop.

4.13

Although professionals recognised the weaknesses of an approach which allowed children to remain with their parents in these circumstances, they had clear reasons for not removing children from their homes.

- Children had strong attachments to their family.
- Research showed that outcomes for looked after children were poor.
- There was a lack of good quality foster homes and residential provision.
- Residential provision would not meet the needs of the child.

Extended family

4.14

For many children, a key aspect of their needs being successfully met was the part played by the extended family, most commonly aunts or grandparents. Where they lived in the neighbourhood, they often provided practical and emotional support for the children and their family, enabling the family unit to be preserved. Where parental ill-health, or the presence of a dangerous partner, made the maintenance of the family unit untenable, in many instances it was a relative who took over care of the children. The ability of these relatives to operate effectively was often seriously constrained, however. In unstable home situations, it sometimes seemed that relatives' availability to pick up the pieces 'at the drop of a hat', and then relinquish care of the child equally quickly, was taken for granted.

4.15

Where relatives took on the long-term care of children they often felt unsupported and their requests for help were not always met. Often there were difficulties in obtaining financial support when children were being looked after by relatives. On occasions, in an emergency agencies moved children to relatives without checking the suitability of the family.

> Marie, a lone parent, cared for her very young nieces and nephews and her own children alone for several months. She had agreed to do so in an emergency. Several months later she had to 'give notice' in writing to the social work department before a determined effort was made to find foster parents for the children. She had been advised by the social worker that it was only by doing this that the case would be treated as a priority because of foster carer shortages.

Foster care

4.16

When, to secure their safety, children were placed successfully in foster care, their circumstances, particularly material and health circumstances, often improved. Schools often noted improvements in the attitude and performance of older children following fostering. If children were accommodated, their health needs were properly attended to and any remedial work, such as treating dental caries, was undertaken. When looked after away from home, children also had opportunities for developmental activities such as joining clubs or having new experiences.

4.17

We also saw cases, however, where foster carers could not cope with the behaviour of children.

> Connor experienced three foster carers within the space of a week who all found it difficult to cope with his disturbed behaviour and extreme levels of distress at being removed from his family. The only solution was to place him with his 18-year-old, lone-parent sister who was pregnant. Whilst his circumstances improved considerably and he was secure, longer-term prospects of security were poor.

4.18

Occasionally, children were sent back home from care, against their will, in one case to a household with a father who had convictions of sexual abuse against children.

Support for children

4.19

For some children, good outcomes were the result of effective anticipation and/or early intervention. Practice was generally better for new babies whose parents had a learning disability, mental health problem or drug problem. Health services arranged for pre-birth or pre-discharge meetings with the other key agencies. These worked well when all the key agencies attended, a multi-agency plan was made and the individual workers each played a part in implementing it. Good work also prevented risks escalating.

4.20

The type of services children and young people needed in order to develop and mature into healthy, well-adjusted adults ranged from immediate practical and emotional support to long-term therapeutic help. In too many instances the case audit found that children were not receiving the services they needed.

4.21

Overall there was a shortage of skilled workers with time to offer children practical and emotional support. We were told that:

- social workers were unable to offer services directly to children or their parents because of a lack of time for regular meetings or because they felt they lacked the appropriate skills; and

- psychology, psychiatry and specialist counselling waiting lists were so long that children could not gain access in a reasonable timescale. Psychological and psychiatric support services would not deal with cases where they recognised a range of other contributory family problems.

> 'Child psychiatry is not an appropriate service. What is required is a stable family environment, and as much support as possible. I do have concerns about David's future, and at any point in time I would suggest that individual work would be an appropriate intervention for him' (Letter from Child Psychiatry unit in relation to 9 year old David who exhibited very disturbed behaviour at school and had sexually abused his little sister).
>
> Aaron had learning difficulties. He sexually abused a fellow pupil but received no help about appropriate behaviour or sexuality. He committed his next offence in a public park, was arrested, charged and by now may have been convicted.
>
> Carl was originally identified pre-school as in need of psychiatric support. By the time he transferred to secondary school, he was described as a danger to his siblings and other persons weaker than himself.
>
> Patrick had shown coercive and explicit sexual behaviour towards other children but though his mother had been asking for help he had been on a waiting list for a specialist agency to address sexual aggression for six months.
>
> '... if social work had more resources and time more work could be done'; 'staffing and workload issues have had significant impact on the service that could be provided to this and other families'; 'as the need for on-going work was identified as being appropriate and necessary it was agreed for this case to be transferred to a more appropriate member of staff. This was, however, not possible to achieve due to staffing shortages'.

4.22

A few authorities provided or directly commissioned therapeutic support from voluntary agencies. Where support was offered, it was valued and made a good contribution to the welfare of children. In some instances individual social workers took the initiative in seeking funding and setting up support groups when they could not access appropriate help for the child. Examples included:

- a group for boys with low self-esteem;
- a group for the children of substance abusers; and
- a service for children with sexualised behaviour.

> **Good practice examples:**
>
> Owen and Margaret's mother had a serious problem with alcohol misuse. They were offered sustained emotional and practical support by a voluntary project that significantly improved their wellbeing.
>
> Following a detailed psychological assessment, a collaborative planned programme was put in place to address Simon's speech, language and numeracy difficulties, his reluctance to eat and to help him develop friendships and self-esteem.

4.23

Overall there was a tendency to overlook the needs of child perpetrators. Nationally there are one or two programmes for young people who exhibit sexually abusive behaviour. Nor were programmes available for children who were showing signs of other damaging compulsive behaviours such as self-harming.

4.24

Generally, referrals to the educational psychology service did not result in children receiving specialist support. Schools told us that the use of educational psychologists as advisers to schools rather than as caseworkers limited the availability of such support for children with emotional and behavioural needs.

Key staff

4.25

Good workers made a real difference to the outcomes for children. In a number of instances, particularly in relation to drugs or alcohol abuse, where strong, supportive relationships had been established between the social worker and the misusing parent, he or she was able to address the problems and was very positive about the support received. In some cases, children suffering from emotional abuse began to respond positively when they developed good relationships with the classroom assistants assigned to them by their schools.

> **Good practice example:**
>
> A health visitor assisted a family of eight children where there were problems of postnatal depression and relationship difficulties. She responded well to the parents' personal and emotional needs as well as their health needs without involving other agencies.

4.26

Often, successful practice in meeting children's needs was due to the approaches, determination and effective work of particular individuals, either from the agencies or in some instances from the extended family. Notable examples of determined and effective work were:

- the social worker who persistently and intensively worked with a drug using mother about the impact of the drugs on her new baby;

- the care workers who, on a daily basis, worked with unskilled parents to gain their confidence, raise their expectations and performance and served as a key line of communication with other agencies;

- the primary headteacher who specifically deployed a classroom assistant to provide 'a haven' for a much neglected pupil;

- the nursery manager who employed a home visitor to support parents who were struggling and to prevent child abuse developing;

- the police officers who supplemented other evidence by searching through supermarket video-camera surveillance footage;

- the relative who spent a whole day, largely unsupported by statutory agencies, with a suicidal mother in order to physically prevent her taking her own life;

- the Reporter who made wide-ranging enquiries to ensure that all the needs of one child were attended to; and

- the health visitor who was persistent in ensuring a child protection plan was made and implemented.

4.27

Good practice in relation to support for children included:

- Support from a named worker to reassure children that their concerns had been addressed.

- Therapeutic services where children had an opportunity to work through what had happened to them, come to terms with it and move towards a different future.

- Remedial health care to address neglected problems such as poor eyesight, dental decay and hearing difficulties.

- Information and guidance about inappropriate behaviour, particularly in cases of sexual abuse or bullying.

- Change programmes that targeted entrenched problem behaviours.

- Foster carers with the level of expertise and skill to care for children whose behaviour was so disturbed that they needed more specialist help.

- Remedial help that provided opportunities to make up for gaps in children's development, in particular those that improved confidence, sense of purpose and self-esteem.

- A sustained relationship with an individual who would 'be there for' a child consistently, spending time with them, listening to them in their distress and helping and supporting them as they developed.

How were families treated?

4.28

The review team had access to very few parents. We interviewed parents in respect of 17 children. The majority of the parents were happy with agency responses and a number spoke highly of the professionals involved with them. In most cases, agencies established good relationships with families in what were often difficult circumstances, but families often felt that they were not kept fully enough informed about what was happening.

4.29

The views of parents were generally well recorded in social work files if they were critical of social work or if parents had sought a change in supervision patterns. Where parents valued social work, or other help, this was rarely recorded.

> Good practice example:
>
> An investigating police officer discussed possible scenarios with her supervisor prior to interviews. She was able to give authoritative responses to children's or parents' questions at the end of the enquiry, without leaving families unsure about what would happen next.

4.30

The children and families in the sample who were of minority ethnic descent came into contact with primarily white British practitioners. The practitioners were all committed to understanding their needs but were frequently concerned about their lack of knowledge about ethnicity and different religions and cultures and were worried about 'getting it wrong'. Interpreters were usually available but there were cases where older children were used to interpret for their parents. In one case an external interpreter adapted the evidence to provide a culturally acceptable translation. Professionals from the statutory sector often used staff from voluntary organisations who worked with minority ethnic groups for providing advice on matters relating to race and ethnicity, especially in relation to domestic abuse.

4.31

Families and children had their own views about successful outcomes which often focused on public punishment of the abuser. Where court cases were not pursued through lack of evidence, or were dismissed, victims felt that they had not been believed. The arrest and imprisonment of offenders was not always a reliable protective measure particularly when the cases of bailed offenders might take a year to come to court. Sometimes, through lack of evidence, cases were not proven. In one case a previously convicted offender was released on bail, pending appeal, without any warning to the victim or her family and he continued to be a threat to them. We were concerned that, in these circumstances, advice was not sought from social work or the police about the appropriateness of bail addresses or the need for any conditions of bail.

4.32

As evidenced from social work files, families sometimes said that agencies' arrangements for monitoring the care of their child(ren) felt intrusive. In these cases social workers helped parents to accept the level of oversight whilst recognising that it was difficult for them.

4.33

There was some variation in agencies approaches to working with families. This was identifiable in:

- practice in making announced or unannounced visits to homes;

- preparing families for, and supporting them through investigations and the child protection case conference or court process;

- providing them with records of meetings and decisions; and

- involving them in the on-going core group discussions.

4.34

Some parents were dissatisfied because their preferred outcome from an investigation, for example removal of a child from the care of an ex-partner, was not considered warranted or to be in the best interests of the child. Agencies experienced difficulties in working with parents where an acrimonious break up left both parties with major suspicions of their ex-partners. The case audit found that investigations were approached differently and in some cases the complaints about a partner's behaviour were treated with extreme caution because the complainant had not acted when the couple were together.

Anne made complaints about her ex-partner's behaviour and was advised that it was her responsibility to protect her children from him. There was no inquiry into his behaviour. Anne was described by social work as extremely unreliable and as having chosen a series of unsuitable partners. Records showed that she was also adept at deflecting attention away from her own behaviour. Nevertheless this did not mean that her ex-partner was not abusing the children.

4.35

Occasionally parents complained to social work about the allocation of particular workers – a single mother, with good reason to be nervous of male contacts, found herself assigned a male social worker, in another case, a parent was assigned a social worker who had been her social worker when she was a child. Complaints were properly responded to.

4.36

We found examples where parents had valued highly the support given. We interviewed parents who found the support helpful even if they wished it had not been necessary. Many had social workers who listened to them about their concerns, directly helped them in parenting tasks and provided much needed material resources.

4.37

In many cases parents were co-operative and able to make use of the support that was on offer. There were a number of cases, however, where parents were either resentful of intrusion, or reluctant to accept support. Nonetheless, in many of these cases effective practitioners had put considerable effort into maintaining a relationship with the parent.

4.38

The key features of effective work with parents were:

- persistence in maintaining a working relationship;

- provision of practical social and emotional support for both parent/s and children;

- provision of feedback;

- clarity about risks and what needed to change;

- flexibility about time and place of meetings; and

- taking decisive action to protect children when necessary.

How were children treated?

4.39

Children who had come to the attention of agencies because of abuse and neglect, particularly if there were a number of cases, experienced contact with a large number of adults from different agencies. In respect of one child, the case audit team had contact with 18 people from different agencies. Contact with a dozen professionals was not uncommon.

4.40

The team met with young people who were very positive about the support which they and their family had received. In these cases a recurring feature was the sustained relationship developed with key staff from one or more agency. This contrasted with other cases where young people referred to the ever-changing set of workers to whom they were supposed to relate. Circumstantial evidence from schools, of major changes in attitude and performance of some children, particularly where they had been moved into foster care, suggest that social work intervention had also been beneficial in these cases.

4.41

The team also met and heard about young people who felt let down by the system. These young people felt they had not been listened to or believed and that their problems had not been addressed. Some children were bitter at being required to return to homes where they did not feel safe. Children who became part of a yo-yo cycle between home and foster care were left with little security or sense of worth.

4.42

Children's perspectives were recorded in some cases. In social work files, if a parent or a child had expressed a view about their treatment by professionals, or the various systems, this was well recorded. There was little evidence, however, of children being asked about their experiences of abuse and neglect. For example, where children spoke to teachers or where professionals themselves identified concerns, agencies referred the case to social workers or the police as a matter of course, according to guidance. We did not find records of either children's views about what should happen with their concerns or of their views about whether the information should be passed onto another agency. In cases of physical or sexual abuse the views of the children were generally recorded as part of the investigation interview process – what happened and how they felt about it. Children, who expressly stated a view about a particular course of action (for example not to prosecute a parent), had their views recorded, but children were not routinely asked what they thought should happen with their concerns.

4.43

In cases of neglect sometimes there were discussions with children about where they wanted to live and when children expressed a view this was recorded. However, their experience of neglect or their views about their day to day life experiences were not recorded. There was no real indication from the files of what children felt about their experiences or the emotional relationships they had with their carers.

4.44

Whilst all the professionals involved with children were concerned for their 'best interests', they often did not consult with children about what their 'best interests' might be. Many children in the sample were too young to express a view, but many were not. A number expressed strong views, usually in a negative fashion, by not co-operating with supervision orders, fighting against them or showing distress with the plans made for them.

4.45

In spite of social workers' efforts to work constructively with children there were difficulties over which they had no influence or control. In one case, a mother persistently threatened her children that 'if they were bad, social work would come and put them into care!' When it was eventually decided that the children should be taken into care and they were removed from their grandparents' home by social workers, they were very disturbed and believed they must have been 'very bad' for this to have occurred.

Outcomes for children

4.46

There had been concerns about the children in our sample in September 2001, and in most cases, the concerns remained at the time of the case audit in the spring of 2002. It was possible to arrive at an evaluation of how the children's needs had been met and to form a view about whether the longer-term plans were likely to lead to reduced risk or improvement in the children's circumstances. However, for most of these children, the long term outcomes remained unknown. Currently, agencies tend not to have mechanisms in place to evaluate the longer-term outcomes for children, nor was it possible for the case audit to do so and this was a weakness.

Good practice examples:

Six-year-old Heather had been sexually abused by a boy. Social Work provided her mother with support, information and materials so that she herself could assist Heather without direct intervention by social work or another counselling agency.

Eight-year-old Mary's mother was suspected of fabricating her daughter's illnesses. Her father had mental health problems and was an arsonist. Excellent interagency co-operation, between health and social work professionals meant that her mother's mental health needs were assessed and work undertaken to improve her self-esteem. Mary's father was banned from the house through a supervision requirement and Mary was given remedial educational and social help to address the problems her 'illness' had caused.

Joint working between the police, social work department and a voluntary organisation enabled three siblings and their mother to be protected from their extremely violent father. There was a full investigation of his behaviour and he was charged, convicted and eventually imprisoned. The children and their mother were provided with safe accommodation with video cameras, alarms and mobile phones. Police and the prison social worker liaised to ensure measures were put in place prior to the father's release from custody. The school was involved in ensuring the children were protected and supervised into the taxi to take them home. Therapeutic resources were also offered.

4.47

In coming to conclusions about cases we focused primarily on whether children were protected and whether their needs were met. We also considered if procedures had been followed and whether the general quality of the work was of a good standard. Of the 188 cases examined by the team we were unable to draw conclusions in 9 cases because of insufficient information. Of the remaining 179 cases we found a number of children (40) were either not protected or their needs were not met following the intervention of agencies. A further 62 children were only partially protected or their needs only partially met. In 77 cases children were protected and their needs were met and in 24 of these cases the needs of the children were well met. Figure 5 on page 92 outlines two case examples in detail. In one case practice was considered to be good and the outcomes for the child were positive in that he was well protected and his needs and those of his family were met. In the other case practice was not good, the child and her siblings were not protected from abuse and neglect and their needs were not assessed or met.

Meeting need and protecting children: Good practice

4.48

Although we could not look at long-term outcomes for children we found that good practice occurred in those cases where:

- the direct provision of help to parents and children was given as and when it was needed;
- there was a helpful and timely response and early thought and preparation; and
- the source of the risk was properly addressed.

Where practice conformed to the above principles children and young people were more likely to be protected and more likely to have their needs met.

4.49

In cases of domestic abuse best practice was seen in those cases where the father's abusive behaviour was tackled and both the mother and children were protected.

Good practice example:

Fourteen-year-old Natalie was a bright young woman at risk of sexual explotation and substance misuse. An extremely sensitive joint interview by police and social work was carried out and a joint meeting between Natalie, her mother and her school guidance teacher arranged. Natalie's mother was caring but had learning difficulties and was not aware of the warning signals or what needed to be done. It was decided that there would not be a criminal investigation, instead a case conference would be held and support would be provided through a welfare support group involving the social worker, guidance teacher and mother. A package of support was put in place to increase mother's knowledge and strategies for dealing with the risks. This was coupled with information and guidance for Natalie and close monitoring of her behaviour by her social worker and education staff.

Children who were not protected or whose needs were not met

4.50

Where children were unprotected or their needs were not met, the failures of the system were either multiple or related to one significant aspect of the case. In most cases a significant weakness was a lack of assessment of a child's needs and many cases also suffered from poor investigations or lack of thoroughness in enquiries.

Fourteen-year-old Andrew was accused on two separate occasions of sexually assaulting young children and there was a further case with a child of his own age. The case was properly investigated by the police and social work and appropriate work undertaken with him to reduce the likelihood of him reoffending. There was, however, no exploration of whether Andrew was or had himself been abused. The school did not undertake a risk assessment of the risks he posed to other children.

Fiona disclosed sexual abuse aged 8 and again at 14. The situation deteriorated and she drifted into prostitution, drink and drug misuse, truanting and self-harm. Eventually she was placed in secure care. Initial allegations of sexual abuse were not properly investigated or followed up and Fiona's mother could not protect her from the abuser, her mother's partner. There were delays in holding a case conference and delays in framing grounds for a Hearing. It was eventually heard under 'non-school attendance'. The abuse was not dealt with and no counselling offered. At the time of the case audit Fiona was due to be returned to the environment from which she needed to be protected.

4.51

Some professionals appeared to have become inured to the circumstances in which some children were living and did not recognise, or did not know how to act on their responsibility to effect change.

Lucy now aged 11, was born into a large family where there were long-standing issues of abuse and neglect including many injuries caused by neglect e.g. cuts from glass on the floor and loss of eyesight due to lack of treatment. There was provision of considerable home care support and a number of professionals were involved with the family. The school was slow to raise concerns. Social work provided help and assistance but did not address the needs of the children individually or collectively. Day by day the children's circumstances continued to deteriorate.

4.52

There were cases where children were not fully protected and their needs were not fully met, but where practice was on a day-to-day level of a good and consistent quality. A feature of these cases was the level of effort employed by agencies, particularly social work services, without an appreciable improvement in children's lives. In these cases a lack of assessment of the parent's ability to adequately care for their children was often a feature.

> Louise's mother had previous children taken into care because of physical abuse and neglect. Louise's father was violent and withheld family finances. He did not help with child care. There were numerous incidents of concern ranging form allegations of sexual abuse, unexplained injuries, general neglect, the presence of unsuitable adults around the children and sibling bullying. Louise's mother was provided with parenting help and the children were in nursery. There was a high level of social work monitoring of the case, home visits were frequent and the children's welfare was monitored closely. But the needs of the children had not been properly assessed and there was no plan to meet them. The case was supervised by a social work assistant whose work was excellent but she was not able to take the overview that was needed. The catalogue of concerns was responded to in a piecemeal way rather than as a pattern.

4.53

In some cases the action taken to meet need and protect a child was appropriate but only taken after a long history of abuse and neglect by which time children were already damaged by their experiences. In other cases all the correct procedures were followed when abuse was identified but the experience of the family and the child was a poor one. Occasionally, in spite of all practitioners' best efforts, a child remained unprotected because of decisions made elsewhere in the system.

Key messages

- Children are often unprotected due to poor assessment of risk and of parental capacity to meet their responsibilities. Some parents receive considerable family support and their parenting abilities are greatly improved but others are unable or unwilling to change despite high levels of intervention.

- Some children's circumstances significantly improve in foster care.

- In too many instances children do not receive the services they need.

- A consistent feature of good practice is the direct provision of help to parents and children as and when they need it.

- Good workers make a crucial difference to the outcomes for children.

Figure 5: Practice Examples

Example of practice 1

Background

One of five children, Claire lived with her mother. Her mother was a drug misuser and convicted drug dealer who had lived with a series of violent partners. She had alleged that she was abused by her father who had convictions for sexual offences against children. She also alleged she had been abused by her brother.

Summary of key events

Aged 1 month: Claire's mother had a new violent partner living in the family home.

Aged 8 months: Claire had a broken arm. Hospital and social work staff accepted her mother's explanation that she fell out of her buggy. Her mum made an allegation that her father had abused one of her older children but she then withdrew the allegation.

Aged 12 months: Claire's mother's partner left and she and her brothers and sisters spent a lot of time at their maternal grandfather's house as her mother found it difficult to cope alone. Further allegations were made against the grandfather but their GP found 'nil of note'.

Aged 2 years: Claire's mother was seen to assault Claire's brother. He was 'pushed to the ground so he hit his head on the pavement'. There was a referral to the Reporter and Claire's Mum agreed to work on parenting skills.

Aged 3-4 years: Claire's mother continually told the school she was unable to cope and was hitting her children. The children were dirty, uncared for and had scabies. There were referrals to social work about 'mother's drug misuse, unsuitable adults, neglect of children's health and the children's disturbed behaviour'. A social worker was allocated, but the case was closed after four months as the social worker had 'rarely managed to meet with mum' and 'mum was stating that she was coping better and had good support'.

Aged 4 years: There were further allegations of sexual abuse of all the children by their grandfather. There was a referral to case conference and the Reporter. Claire's mum took an overdose and Claire and her siblings were removed from the maternal grandfather's to an aunt's home.

Aged 5 years: The children were moved to foster carers as their aunt could no longer cope with them. All the children were displaying very sexualised and disturbed behaviour.

Comment

Early allegations of sexual abuse by the grandfather were not investigated.

When Claire's arm was broken, her mother's story was accepted without consideration of her partner's history and the police were not asked to investigate.

The medical examinations of the children following allegations of sexual abuse were undertaken by the GP rather than a specially trained paediatrician. There was no forensic examination. The police did not interview those who disclosed the information or the grandfather. Police did not check the grandfather's criminal record (which included sexual offences against children) until after the case conference.

The children's needs or their mother's capacity to meet them were not assessed until they were removed from home.

The concerns of neighbours and the school were not properly investigated by social work or properly responded to.

The children did not receive help to meet their needs and were not protected from potential abuse by their grandfather or evident abuse and neglect by their mother or her partner.

Example of practice 2

Background

Duncan was born withdrawing from drugs. He was of low birth-weight. Both his parents were addicted to heroin and were on a methadone programme pre and post Duncan's birth.

Summary of events

Immediately after his birth Duncan was placed on the Child Protection Register as at risk of physical neglect. He was referred to the Reporter and placed on supervision.

Duncan's father was imprisoned on drug-related matters soon after his birth and on his release from prison (when Duncan was 4 months) he was violent towards Duncan's mother. There was a further incident when he and friends were misusing drugs in Duncan's mother's home and the couple subsequently ended their relationship.

Agency involvement

Duncan's mother was in contact with specialist drug misusing pregnancy services prior to his birth. A multi-agency pre-birth case discussion identified all the risks to Duncan and began planning how these might be reduced.

The plan provided both support and monitoring.

Monitoring included:

- observation of mother (and father at times) and her interaction and care for Duncan by the health visitor and social work staff;
- monitoring of drug misuse (as mother was breast feeding) through urine analysis;
- 'on spec' home visits by the social worker to 'check out' who was there and what was happening in Duncan's home;
- monitoring of Duncan's development and health by the health visitor, GP and social worker.

Support included:

- home care support provided by social work services to help Duncan's mother develop routines and care for him;
- support and counselling for Duncan's mother in her methadone reduction and drug withdrawal programme and counselling by the drug misusing clinic and the social worker;
- direct social work with Duncan's mother on childcare, the break up of the parental relationship, social isolation, developing parenting skills and managing a home;
- work with Duncan's father on his parenting role and he was also offered a place on an offending behaviour programme;
- the provision of accessible information by the social worker to Duncan's mother on the effects of drug misuse on the children, particularly through breast milk or the secondary inhalation of heroin smoke.

Good Practice

The comprehensive inter-agency plan for protecting Duncan's welfare was agreed prior to birth and implemented from the day of his birth.

Both parents were fully engaged in the process, attended all meetings and were supported in doing so.

All practitioners (midwives, health visitors, paediatrician, social worker and drug misuse workers) kept a clear focus on Duncan's needs whilst ensuring his mother had all the support she needed to make changes to her lifestyle.

The social worker's recording was meticulous. It focused on Duncan – his growth, developmental milestones, relationship with his mother, health and environmental circumstances. The reports for the Hearing were of an excellent quality providing social, personal, health and other information on which good decisions could be made.

Observation

In this case the social worker was pivotal in the network of professional support surrounding Duncan. Her practice was excellent and a model for good practice in working with drug misusing parents. The other professional staff supported the social worker in her role and *together* they achieved positive outcomes for both Duncan and his mother.

Figure 6: Summary of effective practice

Recognition and referral
All professionals working with children can identify signs of abuse and neglect and know how to respond.
Referring agencies produce a written referral detailing the circumstances, behaviours or incidents of concern.
Social work and the police respond promptly to concerns.
Effective investigations and enquiries
Full gathering of information from all relevant sources.
Potential crimes are investigated thoroughly by the police, using rigorous evidence collection for example taking DNA samples and reordering for evidence to corroborate the accounts of children, parents and suspects.
When examining the presenting injury doctors seek full medical information, particularly previous accident and emergency visits, and take account of a child's social history.
Social workers seeking and taking account of the previous history of any child in need and all relevant information held by other agencies.
Interviews of children are sensitive to their needs.
Medical examinations identify health care needs and are not used soley for evidence gathering purposes.
Assessment and planning
Agencies use well-structured assessment frameworks that provide for: <ul><li>detailing the behaviour(s) or incident(s) of concern;</li><li>assessing the child's needs (including for protection);</li><li>assessing the parent's ability to meet them; and</li><li>detailing action needed to reduce risk both in the short and long-term and to meet the wider needs of the child.</li></ul>

Case conferences
Case conferences are held timeously and minutes are circulated promptly.
All participants are clear about the purpose of the meeting, the process being followed, how decisions will be made and the conference recorded.
All individuals and organisations with information to contribute attend and share accurate information openly.
Discussion and minutes distinguish between facts, inferences and assessments.
Children and parents are fully involved as far as is possible and appropriate.
Protecting children
Direct provision of help to parents and children given as and when needed.
A helpful and timely response and early thought and preparation.
The source of risk is properly addressed.
Support for children
Individual support according to need.
Children are supported, reassured and kept informed by a key worker throughout the process of enquiries or investigations.
Services are provided that offer, as needed: <ul><li>information and guidance;</li><li>change programmes;</li><li>personal or family therapy;</li><li>skilled foster care;</li><li>reparation of harm and missed developmental needs;</li><li>remedial health or education services; and</li><li>a therapeutic relationship.</li></ul>
Partnership with parents
Attempts to maintain a working relationship are persistent.
Social, practical and emotional support is provided.
Feedback on parenting is provided (to fathers as well as to mothers).
Parents are given a clear statement about the child's needs and what must change.
Arrangements for meetings are flexible to meet parental requirements.
Decisive action is taken where necessary.

"It's everyone's job to make sure I'm alright."

What leads to success

5.1

Throughout the case audit we saw many examples of good practice. Figure 6 on page 94 provides a summary of effective practice.

The nature of the problem

5.2

When the fieldwork element of the case audit was completed, we examined the emerging global picture of agencies' practice and the outcomes for children.
We considered whether practice and outcomes might be affected by:

- the degree of deprivation in the area;

- urban or rural location; and

- the complexity of problems facing families.

5.3

We found that children remain unprotected across both urban and rural areas and across areas of deprivation and areas of relative affluence. Doing well was less frequently evidenced in poorer urban areas, although we found sufficient examples to conclude that it was possible to do well even in the most difficult socio-economic environments.

5.4

The level of problems in a family's life did not appear to affect how well agencies performed, but it did appear to be much more difficult to do well if there was a sex offender living in the family or in close contact with the family.

5.5

We found that the outcomes for children were highly dependent on social work doing well. Where social work performed well, the outcomes were generally good and when they performed less well the outcomes were poorer. Good outcomes were assisted by the work of all agencies, but were less dependent on other agencies.

Resources

5.6

As part of the review we asked staff to log time spent on their activities. Some cases required very little professional input but these were generally cases where no further action was needed after an investigation.

5.7

Most of the children and their parents needed, and were receiving, considerable help from a range of services or were continually coming to the attention of the police or social work. We considered if doing well with difficult cases required a higher level of resourcing. It was very evident that complex, chronic or acute problems required a high level of staff resources from a number of agencies but the level of resources did not appear to be a significant factor in the quality of work. Those cases that were well managed required no more resources than many of the cases that were poorly managed. Some cases which were not allocated designated workers and where decisions had been made not to invest in the family, often took up as much agency time as those cases that had planned sustained interventions. More noticeable, were the different patterns of resource use.

5.8

In good practice cases where there was substantial agency involvement, there was always a skilled social worker who assessed the child and family's needs and who was actively working with the parents and others to change the circumstances for the child. In these cases the social worker had more direct contact with the child and parents and other social care staff, such as home carers, often had less. Other resources were used judiciously for specific purposes and overall the resource use was no higher. In these cases the involvement of other professionals in the work plan was also generally high but, again, in a more focused way and no higher than in those cases that were less well managed.

5.9

In well managed cases time was spent on communicating with other agencies by all practitioners but this was not unduly time consuming, other than in the initial development of the professional network. It was also noticeable in these cases that social workers spent time consulting with other professionals and their line managers and in thinking and planning.

5.10

Better practice was noted with new born babies where planning started before birth and was multi-agency. In these cases there was often as much activity pre-birth as immediately post birth. Clearly it is easier to plan and reflect if a situation is not in crisis and we saw some good examples of professionals acting in anticipation of increased risks.

5.11

These findings might suggest that the key to efficient and effective use of resources lies in:

- anticipation, thinking, planning, reviewing and oversight by all agencies;
- working with families as soon as risks are identified; and
- direct social work with children and their families.

5.12

There are a number of vacancies in children's services across all disciplines as Table 2 shows.

Table 2: Staff vacancies

	Number of staff in post	Number of vacancies	% of vacancies
Social workers	1,643	197	10.7
Health visitors	1,362	64	4.5
Educational Psychologists	354	25	6.6
Consultant Paediatricians – Community Child Health – Hospital	28 104	5 10	15.2 8.8
Consultant in Child and Adolescent Psychiatry	59	4	6.3

All figures relate to 2001 apart from those for health visitors which are for 2002.
The figures are Scottish Executive statistics which have been provided by local agencies. They are not up to date and are indicative only. Some of the figures for numbers of staff are whole-time equivalent figures.

5.13

Figures on the numbers of posts, or any vacancies, in Sure Start and other programmes are not collated and numbers of police vacancies are held only at local level.

5.14

Different agencies responded to resource constraints in different ways. During the review agencies told us that the lack of psychologists, psychiatrists and counselling services led to the agencies providing these services refusing new cases or maintaining waiting lists. Social work services generally prioritised cases according to a hierarchy starting at the top with children in need of protection, followed by looked after children, children living at home and supervised by the local authority and finally, other children in need. The police, during staff shortages, generally prioritised child protection work and filled posts from other sections. They therefore responded to all 'child protection' referrals quickly and promptly but resource constraints affected the depth of subsequent investigations or the skills of those undertaking them.

5.15

Almost all the agencies prioritised children who were considered to be at risk and describing a child as 'at risk' generally resulted in a more immediate response from agencies. One agency's system for prioritising referrals or cases was not always shared with partner agencies whose staff only became aware of a formal or informal systems operating when difficulties in obtaining a service occurred. For example, in one area Reporters only became aware of social work prioritisation systems when chasing up late reports.

5.16

Both the general lack of social work resources for children and social work vacancies were cited by professionals as reasons for poor performance. It was very evident that few social workers had time to work directly with children and their families and this is noted throughout the audit.

5.17

Social work vacancies were attributed to the unattractive nature of working with children and families in a hostile public and press climate and the migration of children's social workers to the voluntary sector or new projects such as new community schools.

5.18

Many local authority social work staff did tell us that it was difficult working in such a hostile climate, but in their day-to-day work it was the lack of opportunities to directly work with children and their families and the welter of procedures and bureaucracy that frequently frustrated them. Many saw the voluntary sector as attractive because it focused on meeting the needs of children and enabled staff to use their core social work skills of working with children and families.

5.19

During the audit we found severe shortages of social work staff in some local authorities and some teams were as much as 50% under staffed. In these teams the quality of work in those individual cases that were allocated was not necessarily affected. We found some of the best practice in the most understaffed teams, but cases might remain unallocated and therefore recieve no service at all. Although staff were very concerned about cases that were unallocated, they were grateful to line managers for ensuring their own workloads were not excessive.

Accountability

5.20

Agencies working in the field of child protection are accountable to the children and families and communities on whose behalf they act, to the other agencies with whom they work and to their own agencies. Not all accountabilities are clearly defined, or regularly assessed. Where they do exist, accountability mechanisms work in different ways in respect of each professional group and each agency and some work better than others.

Parental and child accountability

5.21

The children and families in the case audit sample needed help to navigate the systems put in place to assist them. Some professionals took a high level of personal and professional responsibility for ensuring that a child was protected or his or her needs met. In many cases the responsibility was an inter-agency one and there was no obvious person of whom it could be said 'the buck stops here'.

5.22

Case conferences demonstrated their accountability to parents by ensuring their presence at meetings and providing them with copies of relevant reports and action plans detailing the work of various agencies. Not all parents had the opportunity of attending case conferences although this has long been considered to be good practice. Even those who did attend often did not receive reports, minutes and plans, or were not given opportunities to respond to them.

5.23

Children rarely attended case conferences and so were unable to use this forum to hold professionals accountable. Professionals exercised accountability for children's welfare through offering services via their parents. They did not always ensure the children obtained those services, however, if parents were unable or unwilling to take them. For example, we saw one case where a psychiatrist closed a case because parents did not bring a child to appointments.

5.24

In other cases, accountability for meeting children's needs came second place to protecting a worker's safety – health visitor services were withdrawn from a family with vulnerable young children following threats to the health visitor; a teacher would not express a view about a child being placed on the child protection register because of intimidation at the case conference.

5.25

There were few mechanisms for ensuring accountability for a child's protection and welfare once an issue of concern had been raised. The structures of agency records did not generally allow for recording the outcomes for children. When we requested information about outcomes, as we did in every case, we received statements that children's names were placed on the register, or a support package had been put in place rather than risks had reduced or needs were met.

5.26

We were concerned that a number of children experienced what we termed the 'round of referrals' with no single individual practitioner taking responsibility for meeting the child's needs or seeking to work together with others to meet them. A number of children in the sample had been referred to services with such long waiting lists that there was little likelihood of them receiving a service in the foreseeable future. Meanwhile, parental or children's hopes had been raised that help would be forthcoming. Having referred to another agency, practitioners did not engage in the work that they expected the other agency to undertake. Social workers, guidance teachers, psychologists and psychiatrists all have some skills in counselling children yet we saw examples of all of these professionals referring children to the others for counselling.

5.27

There is no doubt that staff are under considerable pressure and this may be the underlying reason for the 'round of referrals' that we witnessed. For the same reason agencies were 'screening out' children for services. A child who might need some help could be subject to an assessment process, sometimes an intrusive or lengthy one, in order to determine whether or not a service would be provided. In many cases an early helpful response to meeting need might well have taken less time than it took to deny the child the service. For example, we saw cases where children as young as 4 or 5 had sexually abused other children. Considerable time was spent by a number of agencies in determining if it was a child protection issue and when it was deemed not to be serious enough to call a case conference, the case was closed. In some cases the parents of the abusing children and the children themselves were offered information about sexual development and appropriate touching and play but in others they were not.

Accountability to referrers

5.28

Relatives, the public and staff from a range of agencies are key to identifying children at risk and seeking help on their behalf. The ParentLine study and the case audit demonstrated how dissatisfied many people are when they refer a child to other agencies. Often they believe that agencies 'do nothing'. We know from the case audit that a great deal of work was undertaken in many cases. We also know that this was not always effective and the child still remained at considerable risk. Referrers, seeing lack of progress and without any feedback on what action, if any, was taken, were left with the impression of their referral having no impact. None of the agencies – health, police, education or social work – had systems for feeding back information to referrers or had determined what information might be appropriate to feed back. Moreover, agencies rarely engaged with referrers in a positive way in order to elicit their continuing support as the eyes and ears of the community in protecting its most vulnerable members.

Inter-agency accountability

5.29

Inter-agency accountability is primarily exercised through application of inter-agency agreements or protocols, the most widely used being the inter-agency guidance for child protection enquiries and case conferences prepared by local Child Protection Committees. Although the structures for case conferences varied, as did the quality of written information provided for the conference and emanating from it, this accountability was generally well exercised. Conferences were held according to agreed timescales, reports were prepared, minutes were taken, plans were made and progress was reported on. The case conference model of accountability was an effective one in ensuring all agencies accounted for their work and supported colleagues from other agencies. There was no mechanism however to hold the case conference process accountable for the outcomes for the child. Child Protection Committees do not exercise such a quality assurance role.

5.30

Other aspects of inter-agency accountability were poor. Individual agencies developed policies and procedures which had a great impact on other agencies, but we were told that these were not always fully negotiated with them.

- Police referred all cases of domestic abuse to the Reporter if there were children involved, leading to an increase in referrals that Hearings could not cope with.

- Education and health framed concerns as 'child protection' in order to access resources for a child.

- Social workers formed their own system of prioritising cases thereby not adhering to Hearings timescales or allocation of cases.

- Hearings or courts ordered supervised contact levels between parents and children that social work could not meet.

Agency accountability

5.31

Most professionals are required to work according to agency guidance and a number of systems and procedures have been devised to support staff in this task. In those cases where children are identified as being in need of protection, staff generally work within the guidelines and follow set procedures, the exception being medical practitioners who exercise individual discretion over the extent of their involvement with other agencies and their communications with them.

5.32

Health visitor and social work staff work within agency monitoring systems. Social work and health visitor staff and some clinicians receive supportive supervision from senior colleagues. The model of social work supervision is a helpful one for professionals working in the field of child protection but sometimes it works better in theory than in practice. At best, one social work service supervised staff regularly at all grades, work was properly recorded, line managers had read files and commented on the work and there was clear evidence of staff and managerial accountability coupled with support for staff undertaking a difficult task. At the other extreme we saw one social work service where there was an absence of recording on some files for over a year, where senior social workers had not examined the files during that period and where there was no evidence on the file or in discussions with staff that there was any managerial oversight.

5.33

The extent to which agencies are able to demonstrate accountability in their work with child protection is questionable. We saw few examples, across all agencies, of:

- routine file case audits or examination of practice against expectations;

- records of discussions with staff by line managers;

- sufficiently detailed records to enable a view to be taken about the quality of work or its effectiveness; or

- monitoring of agency practice or reporting mechanisms for senior managers.

Performance management and quality

5.34

Few managers have performance information specifically about child protection activities. The police have outcome targets and information about the levels of arrests, prosecutions and convictions but information about child protection or child safety matters is subsumed within wider categories such as road accidents and assaults. Health services have health outcome targets for children, some of which may relate to abuse or neglect, for example, dental caries are associated with poor diet and education has outcome targets such as the qualifications achieved for children who are looked after.

5.35

The information provided to senior managers about cases of abuse and neglect is usually about:

- the meeting of time targets (e.g. response times, waiting lists, time intervals in the hearing system);

- the volume of work (e.g. numbers of offence investigations, cases or hearings); and

- outcomes of decisions (e.g. prosecution/conviction, supervision orders, names being placed on the child protection register).

Very little information is provided about the outcomes for children or the quality of work.

5.36

Occasionally managers at the most senior level engage in discussions about quality and outcomes and also review the work of their staff. We found examples of social work service senior managers inspecting (or commissioning inspections) of child protection cases and these being discussed at senior management meetings.

5.37

The lack of clear performance expectations was an issue raised by the Consultative Group as an area of concern (see Chapter 7). We asked members of the group to bring examples of agency performance indicators. Many organisations did not have any and no agency had a package of indicators from which their agency could give a clear account of their agency's performance in protecting or helping children.

Key messages:

- Good child protection work is dependent on individual professionals, social work, education, police, medicine and nursing, making judgements, working for the best interests of the child, and being held to account for their work.

- Effective work by all agencies, depends on their working well together.

- Agencies are not good at informing people about the outcome of enquiries or referrals.

- Agency practice lacks regular and rigorous management oversight.

- Agencies lack well developed systems of internal monitoring and accountability.

"It's everyone's job to make sure I'm alright."

The views of children, parents and the public

What do children say about the risks they face?

What do children do when they need help?

What do adults do when they have worries about a child?

How well are children protected?

Key messages

6.1

The previous chapters described the findings of the case audit of practice. This chapter considers what children, parents and other adults have to say about child protection. If it is 'everyone's job' to protect children then we need to listen to the views of children and young people, parents, and members of the public who all have important things to say on the subject. The information in this chapter is based on our analysis of:

- 217 contacts with ChildLine Scotland.

- 21 interviews with young people with experience of the child protection system.

- 100 calls to ParentLine Scotland.

- MORI's analysis of information from eight focus groups (each comprising eight to 10 members of the public).

6.2

The views which are presented in this chapter are those of the children or adults who took part in these studies. The full reports of the MORI study, ChildLine study, ParentLine study and Messages from Young People studies can be viewed on our website at: www.scotland.gov.uk/childprotection.

What do children say about the risks they face?

6.3

More than half of new calls to ChildLine Scotland relate to physical abuse. The physical abuse which drove young people to contact ChildLine during the period we monitored was often very serious. Callers reported that they had been physically assaulted with weapons and had often sustained serious injuries. Most physical assaults were carried out by parents.

6.4

Forty per cent of the calls to ChildLine were about sexual abuse. Many callers reported that they had been seriously sexually assaulted or raped. Most sexual abuse reported was by fathers or other male relatives but some children reported that they had been sexually abused by other young people or neighbours or, in a minority of cases, by strangers. Very few young people reported that they had been sexually abused by a female.

> Dad hit me with a golf club.
>
> Mum hits me with dog leads.
>
> Dad held a knife at my throat.
>
> She punches me in the stomach, she kicks my legs.
>
> He tried to rape us.
>
> She touches me ... feels me down below.

6.5

Only small numbers of children who rang ChildLine Scotland during the study period reported that they had been neglected or emotionally abused. Some of those who did ring about neglect spoke of being left alone. Others reported that they were hungry; or described their homes as dirty.

6.6

Many children who rang ChildLine were experiencing more than one form of abuse. Children and young people often cited parental alcohol or drug misuse, domestic abuse or break up of their parents' relationship as causing or at least contributing to the abuse or neglect.

6.7

Children and young people described the ways in which the abuse or neglect had affected them. The experience of being abused had led to them getting into trouble, becoming aggressive, running away, wanting to be in care, getting pregnant, feeling suicidal or inflicting self harm upon themselves.

> They stick needles in their arms and they drink – I think they are alcoholics.
>
> I don't want to go home, he said he'd batter me and my mum wouldn't stop him. I want to live in a home.
>
> I feel like killing myself.
>
> I've missed three or four periods, I think I'm pregnant.

What do children do when they need help?

6.8

The child protection system as professionals know it may not mean much to children. We know from research that children and young people often suffer abuse in silence. Almost a third of young people in a large study by the NSPCC (Cawson *et al* 2000; Cawson 2002) had never told anyone they had been abused and a further 28% had not told anyone at the time.

6.9

ChildLine is often the first point of call for many children and young people who need help. Many of the children and young people who contacted ChildLine during the project period said they found it difficult to tell others. They were prevented from telling someone for a variety of reasons. Many of them had a sense of responsibility about what disclosure might do to their family. They were particularly concerned where the abuser was their mother's husband or boyfriend.

> I want to tell but I can't find the words.
>
> I tried to tell my boyfriend but I couldn't.
>
> I don't want my mum to know because I don't want them (mother and partner) to separate. My mum is very happy now.

6.10

Some young people were worried that they would not be believed. Their fears appeared to be justified since a number of young people told ChildLine counsellors that they had tried to tell someone, usually a parent, but occasionally a professional, but they had not been believed.

> The worst thing that could happen if I talked to my mum would be that I wouldn't be believed.
>
> I told my mum but he denied it and she believed him over me.

6.11

Only 29% of children and young people who called ChildLine had shared information, and in many cases this was with a friend. In some instances it was a friend who made the initial contact with ChildLine. Young people normally described their friends as very supportive. When children considered 'telling' someone about the abuse, they were normally talking about telling a friend or other family member rather than a social worker, police officer or teacher.

6.12

There was considerable reluctance to inform statutory agencies about abuse. Some young people saw schools as a more user-friendly point for referral than social work or police, but others reported that they were given little support when they approached teachers. A couple of young people did consider approaching child protection agencies following their discussions with ChildLine counsellors. For example, one boy stated that he would now call the police and have his father charged.

> I want it to stop but don't want the social services to know.
>
> They (the police) don't care about you ... they wouldn't do anything.

6.13

It is of concern that boys are less likely than girls to consider calling ChildLine when they need help. ChildLine carried out a large survey in schools and found that 89% of girls would be prepared to ring them, but only 43% of boys would do so (Macleod and Barter 1996). In our study there were fewer ChildLine contacts from boys (41%) and the boys who did ring were less likely to have told anyone that they had been abused. Our study included more calls from boys than ChildLine's own studies have done, however.

6.14

More worryingly, is the fact that ChildLine Scotland are able to answer only 48% of calls which are made to them (ChildLine statistics). Whilst many of the unanswered calls will be children trying for a second or third time, this figure reflects a great unmet need.

What do adults do when they have worries about a child?

6.15

The role of child protection agencies appears to be reasonably well understood by the public as evidenced by the MORI research. However, although social work followed by the police, were cited as the main agencies, the names with which people were most familiar were not necessarily those agencies or people who could help. For example 'Children in Need' (the fundraising event) and 'Esther Rantzen' were mentioned.

6.16

Some people had reservations about what might be involved if they were to contact social work. Most seemed to assume that if they reported abuse a child would be taken away. They were, therefore, very concerned about 'getting it wrong', particularly in cases of sexual abuse. Some respondents said they would have been reluctant to refer to the police or social work services but would happily have spoken to a doctor in the belief that the information about abuse would be kept confidential. Others said they would be more comfortable approaching schools than the social work department.

> It's a criminal offence so you have got to substantiate what you think and you could be the one responsible for the social services deciding to take the child away.
>
> To say nothing of the possibility that if you've got it wrong, the question of libel. It's a possibility.
>
> That the child will be taken away from parents ... that is an awful responsibility really. If you happen to have made a mistake in your assessment.

6.17

This reluctance to contact statutory agencies is confirmed by recent research undertaken by the Scottish Executive on 'disciplining children' where around a quarter (28%) of parents of children under 5 years of age said they would seek advice about their child's behaviour from a health visitor and only 15% of parents of school-age children said they would seek advice from a teacher (Scottish Executive Central Research Unit 2002). No parents mentioned either social work or the police as agencies to whom they would turn. Most parents did not think that how they disciplined their children was a matter for anyone else outside the family.

> I would go to my doctor and tell him about it, if it was my sister (whose children were being abused) I would tell him about the situation and see what he advised.
>
> The likes of the hospitals and stuff should be the first to act ... I don't mean go over the top and get the police involved and stuff.
>
> I would go to the school and say I seen Jimmy Bloggs in the supermarket with his mother and I think she's a bit out of order here.

6.18

Some people who took part in the MORI study felt that in cases where a child looked abused or neglected it was the responsibility of schools and hospitals to pick up on this and act accordingly. While they felt that schools had an important role to play they saw child protection less as a role for mainstream teachers and more for staff specially allocated a guidance role.

6.19

There were mixed views on the role the public should play in child protection. Some people commented that recollections of the James Bulger case would motivate them to act. Some people felt that everyone in a community had a responsibility to keep an eye on children. On the whole, however, people tended to be more willing to act when they knew the person involved. Where a stranger was involved they felt that it would be more difficult to act. Men over 50 said they would be particularly reluctant to do anything for fear of approaching women and children and some commented that action would be more appropriate if instigated by a woman.

> You've always got that (the James Bulger case) in the back of your mind ... I could never live with myself ... I think I would have to do something.

6.20

While people were generally willing to act, the results of the MORI study indicated that they may have found gaining access to help problematic. Worryingly, many respondents, in searching for telephone numbers in a directory, said they would have searched for 'social services' or the 'NSPCC' rather than social work services or Children 1st, as these services are known (and found in telephone directories) in Scotland. A national helpline number was a popular suggestion for improving access to help.

> I actually was helping someone trying to look up a telephone number for one of these type of agencies and it was a nightmare, go to the yellow pages, look at this bit, go to that bit, go to another bit. Now these things surely are important numbers.
>
> ... if you see somebody breaking into a house you know to go to the police, if you're concerned about a child you don't really know what to do.
>
> I think there are too many agencies for irrelevant things. You don't know where to go for help. What help is provided and who is it for?

6.21

The ParentLine Scotland data indicated that parents, relatives and neighbours who had concerns about children knew of the statutory agencies' responsibilities for child protection. They knew how to access them and many had already done so. This might suggest that when concerns become particularly acute, people will find out how to make contact with agencies designed to help.

6.22

A number of those who contacted ParentLine Scotland were doing so because they were frustrated with the response they had received from the statutory agencies. In contrast to the general public's perception that a referral to the police or social work services would result in immediate separation of a child from his or her family, most of those who contacted ParentLine Scotland were concerned about a perceived lack of activity on the part of statutory agencies. In particular, they were concerned about lack of feedback after they had referred a concern. For example, a woman whose daughter had been sexually assaulted said she had repeatedly phoned the woman in charge of the case at the Child Protection Unit only to be told that she was too busy. Further attempts at contacting someone of a higher authority had been met with 'a blank wall'. She said she was becoming more and more frustrated and upset and finding it more and more difficult to stop her partner from taking matters into his own hands.

> Social work have let us down.
>
> No one will listen.

6.23

For those adults who had not already been in touch with child protection agencies such as social work or the police, an important part of the ParentLine Scotland process was exploring their concerns. Callers were reluctant to contact child protection agencies for a number of reasons including:

- fear of the impact on the child or family concerned;

- fear of retribution; or

- concerns about involving social work.

6.24

Some people wanted advice about whether it was possible to make an anonymous referral. Some had already decided to make a referral and wanted a counsellor to tell them that this was the right thing to do. Others decided to make a referral after speaking to a counsellor. One caller said she was reluctant to inform child protection agencies that her daughter had been sexually abused by her father, because her daughter said she did not want her father charged. Her daughter did not want police or social work to know and refused to talk about the abuse.

6.25

Males appear to feel less able to act when they are worried about a child than females. Males made fewer calls to ParentLine Scotland and the reluctance of older males to act was confirmed by the MORI study.

How well are children protected?

The views of children

6.26

Some children who rang ChildLine indicated that reporting abuse to the statutory agencies was protective. For example, one boy said he was now feeling 'great' as the police had been very helpful and supportive and were now going to proceed with an investigation. Many children and young people indicated that they were glad they had told someone they had been abused. A girl who had told her teacher said she felt like he was someone who 'knew the answers'. She said she felt good that someone knew and that there was someone who could take her problems away.

> I felt that they would do something to make my life better and they did and I feel happy now.
>
> I feel happier because I've told folk about it and it has been dealt with.

6.27

Occasionally however, children indicated that they were more vulnerable after reporting an incident. One boy said his father had been charged with assault but he had not been away for long and when he came out the abuse started again. He said his Mum was now too scared to phone social work or the police but they would not do anything without her permission.

6.28

Messages from the young people who were interviewed for the review were mixed. Some young people felt they had been protected and were glad they had told. Others quite clearly felt that they had not been protected because their abuser had not been prosecuted. A number of young people who had become looked after now felt protected and safe but a small number of interviewees felt they were not protected in residential care. They said they were safe from the person who had abused them but were now vulnerable to other forms of abuse.

> Being in foster care protected me from getting into trouble.
>
> Secure accommodation ... made me feel safe and happy 'cause I couldn't get out to run away. It stopped self-harm.
>
> I was safe in secure (accommodation) in the sense that I was away from prostitution, but also in secure I was in with thieves, molesters and drug pushers so I didn't feel safe or protected.

6.29

Significant numbers of children and young people in the ChildLine and Messages from Young People studies described feeling distressed and upset at the way the child protection system had treated them. They felt they had been 'abused' by the very system which was supposed to help them. One girl said her social worker had not told her that she was being taken to foster carers. She had been picked up by strangers '... and I'm not safe with *them*' and had not been allowed to go home and collect her teddy bear or her clothes. Another girl said she had been very distressed because she had been examined by a male doctor. She felt she should have been given the choice of a female doctor. Another girl said she was frightened about going to court, she said she had had vivid nightmares about having to see her parents in court. Other research studies have also found that children are often frustrated by the way in which they are treated by the child protection system and many feel they have not been protected because the abuser was never prosecuted (Taylor *et al* 1993; Roberts and Taylor 1999; NCH Action for Children 1994).

It might have been better if he'd killed me, at least then he'd be in prison.

I wasn't protected, child protection is only words, it doesn't really mean anything.

Nothing happened to the abuser and I think he might abuse other people. He probably has already. The process was not helpful at all and if I knew then what I know now I would never have told.

Adults should keep their promises. I was told I wouldn't have to see my dad in court and he was there laughing.

The views of parents

6.30

It was in the ParentLine Scotland study that concerns about the system's ability to protect children were most strongly expressed. A number of callers were using the service because of their negative experience of seeking help to protect children from the statutory agencies, particularly social work services and the police (in cases where the abuser was not prosecuted).

6.31

In cases of separating or divorcing parents, where perhaps it is difficult to assess if a call is malicious or an expression of real concern about a child's safety, callers often feel children have not been protected. A father claimed the police were slow and ineffective when he had phoned to inform them that his ex-partner was drunk and incapable of looking after their children. He also felt the social work department had been ineffective. He said he wanted to protect his children but he did not know how. A mother said she had had contact with her GP, health visitor and a social worker but felt that none of them believed her 2-year-old son was in danger when he was with his father, even though they had acknowledged he had a bruise and his character had changed.

6.32

There were many more examples of calls where the caller alleged abuse by an ex-partner and indicated that the child had not been protected by statutory agencies. There were only a few calls where parents felt their child had not been protected where the abuser had been someone other than a parent. One woman said she felt the authorities protected the abuser and not the victim. She said the police and social work had not been able to do anything when her son had been sexually abused by another boy. She had now contacted a solicitor because she wanted to take out an 'injunction' (interdict). Another call was from a father whose 9-year-old daughter had been abused by a man in the community. He was angry that the police had not been able to proceed with the case particularly as he said he knew of other incidents involving the same man.

6.33

Most of the other calls to ParentLine Scotland indicated implicitly that the abuse, particularly sexual abuse, had stopped. Therefore, taking action by contacting statutory agencies had some effect, if only to warn the abuser away from the identified child. Where callers, particularly parents, were upset, it was usually in relation to the absence of ongoing help for the child and the family. For example, a woman whose 9-year-old son had been sexually abused had been informed that no professional counsellors were available; a woman whose 10-year-old daughter had been raped had been informed that counselling would not be available until nearer the time of the court case.

The public's perception

6.34

The respondents in the MORI study were aware which agencies might be best placed to assist a child but they were not confident that help would be forthcoming. None of the respondents expressed confidence in the system and the majority felt that agencies did not work effectively together.

We have a thing in Scotland; Children's Panel but I don't know what they do.

There's so many cases where major bodies that are supposed to be organised and have the appropriate information and authority to deal with it, and yet so many of them are falling down, so you sometimes wonder if the child protection in that particular area is as good as it might be.

People in charge should be seeing that all the cases that come before them are properly scrutinised, the proper solution is arrived at and the proper action is taken and I think that in these three areas, that is not always the case.

If all the agencies worked closer together I think it could work a bit better.

In the likes of 'ChildLine', you've got the social work going in, you've got the Children's Panel going in, I mean I would say that's too many pokers in the fire. One would be saying one thing, one would be saying another, and another would be saying another – they're not coming in agreement – they should be for the kid, for the child.

I think there are too many agencies for irrelevant things. I think there's so much bureaucracy. I think its just taken out of proportion. You don't know where to go for help. What help is provided, and who is it for?

Key messages

- Many children do not tell anyone they are being abused or neglected and when they do tell they normally tell a friend, not an adult and particularly not a professional.

- Boys are less likely to seek help when they have been abused.

- When children seek help from agencies they seek help from ChildLine but ChildLine Scotland are only able to answer 48% of calls.

- Adults, particularly men, are often reluctant or anxious about contacting child protection agencies when they have worries about a child.

- Young people and adults are often critical of the service they receive from child protection agencies.

- The child protection system does not always protect children and young people.

Chapter 6: The views of children, parents and the public

"It's everyone's job to make sure I'm alright."

Findings from research and consultations

7.1

So far in this report we have outlined the findings from the case audit and have considered the voices of children, parents and the public. In this chapter we draw together other elements of the review and summarise the findings.

Comparing our findings with research findings

7.2

Our sample of cases was comparatively small. It covered a wide range of issues from more minor concerns about a parent's temporary difficulties in coping with their child's behaviour to serious life-threatening cases of abuse and neglect. In drawing conclusions from these cases we have paid particular attention to how our findings fit with what is known about abuse and neglect from research and other reviews.

7.3

The reasons why children were not protected in our sample were similar to the reasons why children were not protected in other research studies. Many of the children in our sample and in previous studies expected the criminal justice system to protect them by convicting the abuser and delivering justice, but only a very small proportion of identified cases of abuse or neglect lead to a prosecution and even when cases do proceed to court there may not be a conviction (Wattam, 1997; National Commission of inquiry into the prevention of child abuse 1997; Grubin 1998; Scottish Executive Justice Department, Justice Statistics Unit court proceedings database). The small number of children in our sample who were involved in the court system indicated, as have children in other studies (Keep 1996; Goodman *et al* 1992) that the court process has a damaging effect on them. Where the abuser is not found guilty they feel they have not been believed and have endured a distressing experience 'for nothing'.

7.4

We found, as have previous studies and inquiries (Munro 1999; 1998; Social Services Inspectorate 1997; Department of Health 1991; Brandon *et al* 1999; Hill 1990; Greenland 1986; Ibbetson 1996; Sinclair and Bulloch 2002):

- lack of information sharing across and between agencies;

- poor assessment processes;

- ineffective decision making;

- poor recording of information; and

- lack of information on significant males;

contributed to many children not being protected.

7.5

We also found, as have other studies that some children experience further neglect or abuse after they come to the notice of child protection agencies (Department of Health 1995; Hobbs and Hobbs 1999; Hamilton and Browne 1999; Waterhouse *et al* 1998). Where children are known to child protection agencies and are 'in the system' there is still no guarantee that they will get the help they need. Only a quarter of children in our case audit received such help and this appears to be a widespread problem (Gray *et al* 1997; Sharland *et al* 1995; Farmer and Owen 1995). It is possible, however, that the outcomes for children might have been worse without child protection involvement. It might also be that, through contact with child protection agencies, children are more readily identified a second time as having been abused or neglected than if they had never had any contact.

7.6

The lack of confidence children have in the child protection system is UK wide. Children are more likely to speak to friends and relatives than professionals when they need help (Cawson *et al* 2000; Cawson 2002).

7.7

In line with other research studies (Green and Mason 2002; Gray *et al* 1997), we found that the needs of child perpetrators are particularly neglected. Like other studies (Sharland *et al* 1995; Cleaver and Freeman 1996; Platt 1996; Shemmings and Shemmings 1996; Thorburn *et al* 1995) we found that parents' needs were not always met in that they felt they were not kept sufficiently informed of the progress of the investigation or case. We found that the systems of support for foster carers, particularly family carers, were weak. The Sykes *et al* (2002) large scale study of foster carers came to similar conclusions.

Lessons from elsewhere

7.8

In order to assist our thinking about what might be the best way to improve services for children who have been abused or neglected we commissioned a seminar of international speakers. A number of papers were presented on different approaches to dealing with abuse and neglect. An overview of the issues highlighted and discussed at the seminar is provided in Appendix B.

7.9

Whilst different countries approach child abuse and neglect and child welfare differently, there are two distinct approaches emerging in the Western world. One approach is exemplified by Canada and Australia (and also the United States and England) and the other by Sweden, Belgium, France, Italy and Germany.

7.10

The Australian/Canadian approach distinguishes between children who are at risk and those in need. There is a strong emphasis on establishing whether an incident is abusive and who the perpetrators are so there is much evidence gathering, investigation and assessments of risk.

7.11

There is a presumption of protecting family life and parents' rights but, in high-risk cases, child protection is the primary concern and this is achieved through high levels of intervention or removal from home. The harm or risk threshold for intervention in a family's life tends to be high. Systems and procedures have been developed to manage this approach including the development of risk assessment tools as the means to screen children away from statutory intervention. The courts have a significant role in decision making and the court system follows an adversarial tradition.

7.12

Children who are in need but are not considered to be at risk are generally provided for on a voluntary basis, often by the voluntary sector, and there are programmes of early intervention to prevent child maltreatment. The services in this sector are increasing.

7.13

The continental Western European approach tends not to differentiate so strongly between risk and needs. Children and their families are provided with help as part of the state's package of welfare to all children and families who need it. There is no child protection system as such, rather, families in difficulty are encouraged to seek voluntary help and there is a strong commitment to birth family preservation. For example, adoption for older children does not exist in France as an option if children cannot be cared for by their parents. The system is reliant on the skilled helping relationship between the professional (social worker, doctor, child psychiatrist) and children and their families. There are few systems or processes to be followed and meeting need or protecting children is dependent on individual professional judgement. Where cases of abuse or neglect are investigated, this is a role for the police and there is a clear separation between this and the helping role of the social worker or medical practitioner. Those parents that cannot or will not change will come within the more formal court-based systems. These are inquisitorial and conducted by specially trained children's judges. The focus on consensus and negotiation remains and removal of children from their families is not generally considered.

7.14

Children can receive services in their own right. Professionals can work with children in confidence. They are not required to pass on information about abuse and parents do not need to be told that their child has requested or is seeking a service.

7.15

There are benefits and disadvantages to the two approaches. The Australian/Canadian approach enables greater consistency between practitioners and means families are able to care for their children without interference unless it is necessary to protect the child. It also enables some attention to be given to prosecuting abusers and thereby protecting other children. It does not, however, focus attention on meeting children's needs and the thresholds of intervention are so high that there may be significant harm caused before help is provided. Some of these problems are offset by the provision of voluntary help. The system is stigmatising and parents do not willingly become involved in it. Staff turnover is high and there are indications that staff find the approach unfulfilling.

7.16

The continental Western European model is highly dependent on good professional skills and consistency is achieved through training rather than guidance or procedures; practice, therefore, may be variable. Practitioners continue to work in a negotiated way with families and abuse may continue whilst this approach is being pursued. Offenders may not be prosecuted and may be free to offend again within their own family or with other families. Whilst the system is avowedly child-focused the needs of the parents are given particular attention and children's needs may get lost in resolving parental problems. In those cases where parents cannot or will not respond, alternative arrangements are needed and measures of compulsion may be required. Families in difficulty view the approach as helpful, and abusive or neglectful parents more willingly accept help and change behaviour. More children and families are offered and accept help. Staff working in the field of child care are well motivated, are held in high esteem in their communities and turnover and 'burnout' is low.

England and Wales

7.17

The approach in England and Wales is consistent with the Australian/Canadian approach although there are some significant differences.

7.18

In England and Wales the 'Quality Protects' programme of improving services to children is at the centre of reducing abuse and neglect. As part of the programme for modernising and improving services for children a 'Framework of the Assessment of Children in Need and their Families' has been developed and has been implemented in every local authority. The Framework is intended to be a multi-agency tool for assessing the needs of children and responding to them, bearing in mind the needs of the child, the child's environment and parental capacity. Along with the framework, training and research findings have been produced in order to encourage a more evidence-based approach to practice.

7.19

A further development in England and Wales has been the development of 'Serious Case reviews'. As part of the Quality Protects initiative, the previous 'Part 8' child protection committee reviews of deaths of children on the child protection register were redeveloped under new guidance as Serious Case reviews. New guidance was issued in 1999 on the conduct of reviews of child deaths and serious injuries in cases of suspected abuse and/or neglect. The focus of the reviews is an analysis of agencies' practice and lessons learned.

7.20

More recently guidance has been issued on the conduct of criminal investigations into abuse, particularly in complex cases. New inter-agency guidance has been issued. The guidance states that in complex cases such as cases of sexual abuse occurring in schools or care homes, a multi-agency approach to the investigation should be put in place from the outset involving the police, social work and appropriate experts such as lawyers and psychologists. The planning and process of the investigation should conform to certain standards and there should be a consistent approach which protects the welfare of children and vulnerable witnesses but also takes account of the need to protect the rights and privacy of alleged abusers. The guidance covers the approach to investigations and their management, managing and sharing information, dealing with the media, support for staff and legal issues. Whilst the police and social work have always undertaken the joint investigation of certain cases, this guidance strengthens the approach and takes a multi-agency strategic approach to the investigation from the outset.

7.21

In Scotland, Lothian and Borders Police, in partnership with other agencies, has developed guidance for local use on historic abuse and this is currently being considered by ACPOS and ADSW for use nationally.

Child deaths

7.22

During 1999 there were a total of 57,799 deaths in Scotland. Of these 231 were boys under 16 and 216 were girls under 16 years of age. The majority of these deaths were health related (358), however, a number related to road accidents (25), fires (7), suicides (24) and Sudden Infant Death Syndrome (33).[5]

7.23

While the UK's overall road safety record is good, our record on child pedestrian safety is one of the worst in Europe, with a death rate that is double Germany's. More than 130 children die in Great Britain each year and over 4,500 are seriously injured while walking or cycling, and two thirds of all accidental deaths for the 5-19 age group are due to road accidents. Children from more deprived homes are more likely to be killed as pedestrians than those from wealthier households.

7.24

In the year 2000, 20 male and 13 female children were recorded as dying from Sudden Infant Death Syndrome in Scotland. A small number of these deaths may have been caused by maltreatment or very poor care. High profile prevention campaigns have been effective in reducing such incidents.

---

[5] The Statistics in this section come from Information and Statistics Division Scotland and the Scottish Executive.

7.25

Death by fires or drowning are sometimes a consequence of leaving children unattended and parents being under the influence of drink or drugs can be a contributory factor in deaths by fire.

7.26

Young males are twice as likely as young females to commit suicide; and many more children attempt suicide or harm themselves deliberately.

7.27

Clear information about the deaths of children is difficult to obtain as statistics are collated and classified in a number of different ways by different bodies:

* information about Fatal Accident Inquiries (FAI) in Scotland, some of which relate to children, is held on 40 local databases;

* some statistics are recorded on a United Kingdom basis, for example, deaths involving fire; other statistics relate only to children under the age of 16 rather than 18; and

* the International Classification of Diseases (ICD) System for coding all deaths does not identify possible child abuse or neglect cases. For example, malnutrition is noted as a cause of death but not how it occurred. Deaths of very ill children may also be identified only as dying from causes relating to their illness whilst, in some cases, abuse, neglect or inappropriate restraint may have been a contributory factor.

7.28

Some deaths of children are reviewed in Scotland. The Procurator Fiscal is responsible for the investigation of all sudden, suspicious, accidental, unexpected and unexplained deaths. The deaths which must be reported to the Procurator Fiscal include : any death of a child from suffocation including overlaying; any death which may be categorised as due to sudden death in infancy syndrome or sudden unexplained death in infancy (SUDI); and any death of a foster child, a child in the care of a local authority or on an 'at risk' register.

7.29

If a death is notified to the Procurator Fiscal, he or she will decide whether to make any further investigations into the circumstances surrounding the death. Once these further inquiries have been carried out the decision may be taken to raise criminal proceedings or to request a Fatal Accident Inquiry (FAI).

7.30

An FAI is a public inquiry into the circumstances of a death, where evidence will be lead by the Procurator Fiscal and any interested parties may appear or be represented. At the end of the inquiry, the Sheriff will make formal findings setting out: where and when the death and any accident from which it resulted took place; the cause(s) of the death and any accident from which it resulted; the reasonable precautions, if any, whereby the death and any accident from which it resulted might have been avoided; the defects, if any, in any system of working which contributed to the death or any accident from which it resulted; and any other facts which are relevant to the death. The Sheriff has no power to make any finding as to fault or to apportion blame.

7.31

Suspicious deaths are investigated by the police and may result in a prosecution of those thought to be culpable. In some cases there are public inquiries, internal agency reviews or reviews commissioned by Child Protection Committees into the role of professionals following the death or serious injury of a child. The Scottish Executive reviews the deaths of all children who are looked after by local authorities.

Child death review teams

7.32

Elsewhere in the world, most notably in Australia and North America, there are systematic reviews of all child fatalities including deaths from road traffic accidents and health-related causes. The aim of such reviews is to learn from them and develop methods of reducing child deaths, from whatever cause. The teams identify hazards that may place other children at risk from neglect, abuse, violence or unintentional injuries. The teams comprise representatives from medicine, law enforcement, public health, social services, education and other relevant agencies. This information is used to prioritise and focus prevention activities and not to establish blame.

7.33

Evidence of their effectiveness is noted in the NSPCC Report *Out of Sight 2001*, the level of preventable deaths reducing by as much as 16% in some states. The report noted that the risks to children in America are similar to those in Great Britain although deaths from firearm incidents are at a much higher level in the United States.

7.34

In England and Wales Child Protection Committees have a statutory responsibility to undertake reviews of the role of professionals in cases of child deaths or serious injury where there are concerns about possible abuse or neglect. Some Child Protection Committees in Scotland have developed guidance and pilot arrangements for reviews of child deaths where abuse or neglect may be a contributory factor.

7.35

The purpose of Child Death Review Team reviews is to:

- establish whether there are lessons to be learned from the case about the way in which local professionals and agencies work together to safeguard children;

- identify clearly what these lessons are, how they will be acted upon, and what is expected to change as a result.

In the UK child death reviews, where they occur, are not investigations into how a child died or who is culpable. Those are matters for Fatal Accident Inquiries and the courts. Similarly, any disciplinary action against staff is a matter for individual agencies.

Deaths of children and young people who are looked after

7.36

The review team carried out an analysis of the circumstances of 50 looked after children who died between 1997 and the end of 2001. Children and young people are looked after by local authorities when they are provided with accommodation, subject to a supervision requirement or subject to a legal order, such as a child protection order or a parental responsibilities order from Scotland or another UK country. When a looked after child dies local authorities are required to submit a report to the Scottish Executive within 28 days. The report is expected to cover the medical and social history of the child and an account of the circumstances of the death. The Scottish Executive is empowered to:

- examine the arrangements made for the child's welfare when the child was looked after;

- assess whether action taken or not taken by the local authority may have contributed to the child's death;

- identify lessons which need to be drawn to the attention of the authority and other agencies; and

- review legislation policy, guidance, advice or practice in the light of a particular case or any trends emerging.

7.37

Young people who are looked after have revealed to researchers that they do not always feel safe. They have revealed that they are at risk of physical, sexual or racial abuse, or at risk of misusing alcohol or drugs, self-harming behaviour or prostitution (Who Cares Scotland). Looked after children have a higher mortality rate than other children. In 2000 there were 478 child deaths out of a total child population in Scotland of 1,062,140, a mortality rate of 0.04%. In the same year 15 looked after children died out of a total population of 11,309, a mortality rate of 0.13%.

7.38

Nearly half (24) of the 50 children whose deaths were analysed were accommodated at the time of their death, most living with foster carers, and 11 of the children had been on the child protection register at the time of their death. In six of the 50 cases the cause of death was related to pre-existing life-threatening illnesses and in a further 14 cases the cause of death was primarily health-related (although two cases were determined to be the result of Sudden Infant Death Syndrome (SIDS) and a further two were related to the young person's drug use and were self-harm related.

7.39

Of the remaining 30 deaths:

- 11 were suicides;

- 10 were drug, solvent or alcohol-related (often as the result of inhaling stomach contents);

- 6 resulted from road accidents;

- 2 were caused by drowning; and

- 1 was a murder.

7.40

The analysis of the social work and health reports undertaken by the Social Work Services Inspectorate and medical advisors indicated that in some cases more could have been done to protect the children. There were some concerns about medical practice. The lack of mental health services for children and young people with challenging behaviour who demonstrated high levels of reckless or self-harming behaviour was also noted.

- In one case of hanging, preventative measures had not been put in place following a previous suicide attempt.

- In an alcohol/drug-related death, poor home leave planning, lack of residential staff skills in this area of work and issues of staff cover when shifts were changing were noted.

- A young child who drowned was in the care of an elderly temporary carer who was unable to 'keep up' with the child. There was no prospect of the child being returned to his birth family and suitable long-term arrangements were needed.

- In the case of one child who died of SIDS, a child protection case conference held pre or post birth would have addressed the parenting capacity of the child's family.

Figure 7: The views of children, parents, the public and professionals.

Public involvement

- All adults should have a duty to protect children and be helped to do so. There should be a national publicity campaign similar to the 'Zero Tolerance' campaign for domestic violence. There should be a national telephone line for reporting abuse.

Parental responsibilities and support

- Parents should have a more active role in protecting children especially in overseeing children's activities. There should be more help for parents by way of support or training and in particular, how to help in cases of family breakdown or parental separation. Improving families' social conditions should be achieved through reducing poverty. There should be more family resources such as children's centres and pre school care. Tackling specific problems, in particular domestic violence and parental drug misuse, should be a priority.

Schools

- There should be more school based educational programmes for children on keeping safe, family breakdown and sexual abuse. Schools should teach children about their rights. Safe routes to school should be established.

Police

- There should be greater oversight of public places through more police on the streets and video cameras.

Offenders

- Hitting children should be illegal. People who offend against children should be banned from any contact with them. The court processes for child witnesses need to be improved along with an improved conviction rate of abusers.

Agencies

- There should be better communication between agencies or a single co-ordinated system. Children should be listened to and their confidentiality better protected. Professionals should be more reliable in keeping appointments and keeping promises. The courts and Hearings should be less formal. Interviewers and medical examiners should be more child friendly. Agencies should give feedback to referrers on action taken.

Resources

- Agencies indicated a need for more resources, improved training and more guidance on inter-agency co-operation. A number also wanted a national child protection register and national standards for child protection work.

Different systems

- Concerned members of the community and some professionals wanted the option of discussing cases confidentially prior to child protection action being invoked.

How children and young people could be better protected

7.41

Children and young people, parents, other adults and professionals presented to the review team their views on how children and young people could be better protected. Their views are outlined in Figure 8.

Child Protection Committees

7.42

A review of Child Protection Committees (CPCs) was undertaken in 2000 (Scottish Executive 2000b). The report concluded that CPCs were viewed by members as being effective when:

- identifying and promoting inter-disciplinary training;

- ensuring inter-agency liaison;

- promoting and developing inter-agency guidelines; and

- promoting good inter-disciplinary practice.

They were less effective in:

- inter-agency reviews of local child protection practice;

- assessing case enquiry issues;

- development of local preventative strategies; and

- reviewing availability of expert advice.

7.43

The findings of this review indicate that the situation remains broadly the same. Child Protection Committees continue to focus on training, co-operation and guidance and pay less attention to quality or practice issues. Recently, a few committees have developed and implemented programmes for community awareness raising and preventative strategies. Others have developed mechanisms for reviewing cases and inter-agency work and two committees have begun to develop approaches to reviewing the deaths of children.

7.44

The review of Child Protection Committees noted that lack of specific resources and lack of senior representatives on the committees were seen as major barriers to taking work forward. A number of respondents felt the committees had little impact on practice although the indirect benefits of training were recognised. Few respondents wanted radical changes to CPCs, other than that they be placed on a statutory footing with more stable funding. The review concluded that improvements could be made within the current structures and guidance should be revised to strengthen the role of CPCs without placing them on a statutory footing. Some work on revising the guidance commenced but has since been suspended awaiting the conclusion of this review of child protection.

7.45

During our work we met with the chairs of Child Protection Committees. They saw a significant role for committees in the future. Child Protection Committee chairs saw scope for:

- a more systematic review of practice;

- better supervision for case workers across agencies;

- improved communication over children at risk with Accident and Emergency departments

- a training budget;

- a national campaign to improve public understanding of child protection; and

- further guidance on confidentiality issues.

7.46

They thought that improvements were needed in the services provided for particular groups of children – those affected by drug using parents, neglect, disability and those in need of psychiatric help.

7.47

There were concerns about the lack of national consistency in respect of child protection guidance and also other matters such as training and awareness raising. Each committee acted independently of each other following their own agendas but valued the opportunity to discuss issues together on a national basis. This review has been the major focus of the group's discussions during the past year and their early contributions informed the process of the case audit.

7.48

Some Child Protection Committees have initiated inquiries when children known to statutory agencies or children on the child protection register have died or have been caused serious injury. A small number have also recently established local procedures and guidance in order to undertake such inquiries should the need occur. Chairs of CPCs have indicated that they would welcome a statutory responsibility for inquiries into incidents of concern and guidance on how these might be properly conducted.

The Consultative Group

7.49

The consultative group tackled, in a structured way, a number of difficult inter-agency issues.

Confidentiality

7.50

Mixed views were expressed about confidentiality. Some members of the Consultative Group, usually those working in the statutory sector, thought all allegations of abuse and neglect should be passed on to statutory agencies to deal with. Some thought there should be 'mandatory reporting' in Scotland as there is in some other countries. Others, most often those working in the voluntary sector, thought that increasing access to confidential services would enable more children and their parents to get help.

7.51

It was acknowledged that confidence in the statutory sector might be improved if referrers, children and parents had more control over the timing and type of child protection investigations and proceedings. There was some support for professionals taking 'a space for negotiation' – pausing after receiving a referral to consider the best way forward for the child, taking account of his or her views and, where appropriate, the views of parents.

7.52

This would allow parents who were harming their children or thought they were at risk of doing so to negotiate with agencies who could help them, through counselling or change programmes, a period of help without their children being automatically reported as being in need of protection. Similarly some professionals would like a 'space' in which to consider with other colleagues from their own or other disciplines how to approach certain problems without automatically following a child protection route.

7.53

Organisations representing children and young people advised us that young people were extremely concerned about the extent of information sharing between agencies and the erosion of their privacy whilst those working in the statutory sector advocated greater sharing of information about children and their family circumstances.

Race and cultural issues

7.54

The consultative group felt that the statutory agencies and a number of the voluntary agencies did not serve the needs of children or families of minority ethnic origin well.

7.55

Practitioners were concerned that they did not always understand different child-rearing practices and they were unsure whether some behaviours such as physical chastisement, care of young children by older children, and under-age marriage/pregnancy were abusive. They were also concerned about the lack of culturally and racially appropriate services and the lack of people with sufficient knowledge of both minority ethnic issues and child welfare and protection in Scotland to provide appropriate training for organisations. Access to appropriate interpretation services was identified as a particular issue of concern.

Empowerment and 'whistle-blowing'

7.56

The consultative group were concerned that less senior staff in organisations, for example, cleaners in hospitals and dinner staff in schools might not be properly trained to deal with concerns or suspicions that they might have about a child. They felt that better information for the general public about child protection processes would improve understanding of what happens after referral and perhaps enable people within organisations to feel more confident about making referrals. They felt the public also need information about action taken after a referral is made so that they could be assured their concerns were being taken seriously.

7.57

The consultative group felt that staff might be dissuaded from raising their concerns about agency or individual practice due to an existing culture of 'not seeing' abuse or because they were worried about what might happen to them or to a child if they disclosed abuse. They felt some staff might not feel able to report more senior colleagues or might not be aware that some behaviour they witnessed constituted abuse because they may not have had any training on the matter. The group felt that positive guidance on how concerns should be addressed and which explained the systems of support available to 'whistle-blowers' would help to create a culture that was child-focused and did not support abusive behaviour.

Performance indicators

7.58

The consultative group asked whether 'protecting children' was about:

- Reducing the number of children who died or were seriously harmed and did this include all children, for example, those killed in car accidents?

- Reduction of abuse and neglect across the whole population or in cases where this had already been identified?

- Improvement in the wellbeing of all of Scotland's children or those who had been identified as being 'in need'?

7.59

They felt that objectives for child protection should be built into children's services plans and be owned by all the agencies with a responsibility for improving the welfare of children. They thought it was important to have national goals and objectives as there was a danger that individual agency objectives might not be in the interests of children overall. There was some support for process performance indicators, for example, the length of time taken for a case to be finalised at a Hearing or court, but it was felt that such indicators should be secondary to establishing whether outcomes for children had improved. They felt that quality indicators such as the new National Care Standards and the *How Good is Our School?* indicators could help raise the quality of practice and felt similar indicators should be developed in child protection work.

7.60

There was concern that some performance measures were unhelpful. For example, the group pointed out that if an aim is to reduce the number of children on the child protection register this might lead to children being taken off the register prematurely. The need to reconcile different objectives was also pointed out. For example, a successful child protection *agency* might be one that generates high levels of child protection referrals while a very successful national child protection *strategy* might reduce overall levels of abuse and neglect and referrals to agencies.

7.61

The consultative group felt that existing targets which relate to the physical and intellectual wellbeing of children, for example:

- reductions of deaths on the roads;

- reductions in infant mortality;

- increases in educational attainment; and

- reductions in levels of poverty

might better indicate the extent to which children are being protected and their needs met than indicators specifically relating to child protection.

Key messages

- The findings of the case audit bear close resemblance to the findings of research studies and other reviews which have looked at child abuse and neglect.

- No country has found the solution to child abuse and neglect but there is much that can be learned from how other countries tackle the issue.

- More could be done to improve the safety of looked after children.

- Members of the public, children and professionals all believe that everyone has a part to play in protecting children.

- Professionals working in the field of child protection have identified a number of areas where improvements could be made.

"It's everyone's job to make sure I'm alright."

Findings, Conclusions and Recommendations

Progress appraised

Hallmarks of an effective service network

Routes to change and improvement

Action that can be taken immediately

Action over the next three years

Proposals for following up this audit and review

Progress appraised

8.1

This audit and review revealed many instances where children were protected from harm or neglect and their welfare was clearly improved by the support and assistance given by agencies – often working together to beneficial effect. Many well-motivated and committed professionals are working in difficult and stressful circumstances and are capably managing high levels of risk. There is no lack of willingness or effort to do a good job and to stand by vulnerable children.

8.2

There is evidence of real progress and improvement during the past 20 years, though it is not always measurable. Professional practice has changed for the better and many children are better protected than they were in the past. Significant changes include:

- joint working between the police and social work services which has produced a much more child-friendly and comprehensive approach to the investigation of abuse and neglect;

- improved liaison between different agencies and exchange of information;

- greater awareness of the risk of abuse and neglect and sharper vigilance by professionals working with children – which can lead to an earlier response;

- more rigorous selection and improved supervision of residential child care workers;

- the regulation of the social work and social care workforce;

- the introduction of the sex offender register and an index of people who are unsuitable to work with children; and

- the development of improved services for child witnesses in the criminal justice system.

8.3

On the other hand, there is clear evidence that:

- many children are living in conditions and under threats that are just not tolerable in a civilised society;

- children, their parents, the public and some professionals often do not have confidence in the system;

- children and their families do not always get the help they need when they need it;

- some children remain unprotected;

- occasionally, disclosure of abuse makes matters worse for a child;

- there is duplication of effort and energies are diverted into meeting system requirements rather than the real needs of children; and

- agencies are not able to always respond effectively to some problems – parental drug or alcohol misuse, domestic abuse and neglect.

8.4

In short, pressure on resources, and sometimes poor management, assessment and decision making, have led to a position where the system does not act quickly or reliably enough to protect children well, or meet their needs.

8.5

The problems are not new, and there is no one way of solving the challenge of protecting children, supporting parents and protecting parents' and children's rights. The multiplicity of child protection and welfare systems around the world reflects debates about what kind of system and what kind of practices would best meet the needs of children and families and meet the universal tensions of:

- state intrusion versus family integrity;

- children's rights to be parented by their parents and their rights as separate citizens;

- compulsion versus voluntarism; and

- investigation of offending and risk versus assessment and meeting of need.

8.6

The audit and review found that even where there is agreement and consensus, practice may be ineffective. This mirrors the findings of the many previous reviews of child protection which have highlighted how difficult it is to achieve change and ensure that good practice is implemented consistently. Why is it so difficult to achieve?

8.7

Although the current system has the potential to protect children and deliver services to them and their families, it has developed characteristics which undermine the full realisation of that potential. Responses to failures or mistakes in protecting children have been to develop more guidance and regulation. Procedures and requirements have snowballed over the last few decades. Although the additions have been implemented with a view to improving the service to vulnerable children and their families, the cumulative effect has been to render the system increasingly cumbersome. Satisfying procedures and processes can hinder early and effective action and can even frustrate good outcomes for children.

- In the face of media criticism, social work practice has become increasingly driven by procedures.

- Categorising a child's experience as a child protection matter has become an end in itself. Too often this results in close monitoring but stops short of specific actions to protect children or meet their needs.

- Guidance and procedures are being used as mechanisms for rationing services. Help may be restricted to that which is required or specified in guidance, and offered only to those children who are deemed to be sufficiently at risk.

- Detailed investigation in order to determine if a concern is a child protection matter has come to dominate action and resources in relation to abuse and neglect.

8.8

This has resulted in a situation where effective service delivery is often as a result of extraordinary efforts by individuals and sometimes despite, not because of, the system structures. Almost all resources are focused on those children whose needs have become so acute that they can no longer be ignored. In the absence of help being offered at an earlier stage, professionals use the Hearings system and the child protection system as routes to accessing services for children they are worried about, increasing the pressures on both systems. At the same time the number of convictions is small and declining and the number of children who are placed on child protection registers is only a small proportion of children who need help.

8.9

Good investigation, good assessment of children's needs and circumstances, together with decisions and action in the best interests of the child, are all hindered by the complex burden of regulation, procedure and guidance that bears down on first-line professionals.

Hallmarks of an effective service network

8.10

According to the latest available research and the findings of this audit and review, an effective service for children who have been abused or neglected would:

- incorporate preventative strategies;

- be part of wider provision of family and child support;

- build on community and family strengths;

- be trusted by children and young people to act in their best interests;

- be easy to access and simple to understand;

- offer help as and when it is needed;

- treat children and parents with respect;

- act quickly and reliably;

- continuously improve its inter-agency work and assessment processes; and

- match resources to children's needs.

8.11

If such a service existed, the majority of parents and children could be assisted early and on a voluntary basis. But it is also clear, from this audit and review and from many other studies, that a small number of parents either will not acknowledge the risks their children face or will be unable to meet their needs. A much smaller minority of parents will deliberately harm their children. A key feature of any effective service will be identification, as early as realistically possible, of cases where children's needs are unlikely to be met by their parents. Excellent assessment practice is critical to this, as is prompt action to meet those children's needs in other ways.

Routes to change and improvement

8.12

This chapter sets out how Scotland could develop such a network of services to better meet the needs of children and to reduce further the extent of abuse and neglect. The Children (Scotland) Act 1995 provides a robust framework for current practice and our proposals for change are consistent with its principles and many of its provisions. The Cabinet Sub-Committee on Children's Services, chaired by the First Minister, is driving forward the better integrated children's services agenda, following up the *For Scotland's Children* report. The findings of this audit and review reinforce the need for that agenda to develop rapidly at local as well as national levels.

8.13

The Children's Services planning arrangements, whereby agencies in a locality plan to meet the needs of all children, are developing gradually. They offer the best means of ensuring all children have the opportunities and help to achieve their full potential whilst those that need specific additional help will receive it.

8.14

Through Sure Start, Social Inclusion Partnerships and New Community Schools, children and families in difficulty increasingly are receiving help through integrated services.

- Preliminary work has begun on a multi-agency assessment framework.

- Drug and Alcohol Action teams and Child Protection Committees are working on reducing the problems arising from parental drug and alcohol misuse.

It must be through these and other inter-agency routes that future responses to meeting needs are planned and delivered.

8.15

Table 3 below sets out the types and levels of support which local authorities, with their planning partners, are bound to consider when developing services for children and their families. Responsibility for the development and the implementation of preventative and protective strategies should rest at the most senior level of inter-agency planning and be led by local authority Chief Executives. Protecting children should not be a separate activity but should be a responsibility of all agencies and part of all agencies' responses to children's needs.

8.16

The scope which local authorities and their partner agencies have for developing services can be summarised as follows:

Table 3: Types and Levels of Support

Prevention	Raising public awareness. Parenting and child care courses as part of the school curriculum. Parenting information/skills development. Community development. Reducing poverty and the adverse effects of poverty. Improving child health. Crime prevention.
Support	School, nursery, health visitor and social work support. Day care and child care. Family centres. Breakfast and homework clubs and after-school activities. Parenting programmes. Therapeutic resources such as post-abuse counselling.
Intervention	Intensive support and monitoring. Foster and residential care. Shared care. Therapeutic resources, behavioural change programmes, medical and other treatment.

8.17

Where there is already good practice, the vision of a well integrated child-centred network of services driven by children's rights is readily achievable. In those areas where practice is less good, more substantial change is needed. Some of the proposed changes cannot be delivered immediately and require further development in consultation with a number of key agencies. The recommendations in the rest of this chapter are divided between:

- action that can be taken immediately to protect children and to improve services;

- action over the next three years and involving further consultation; and

- proposals for following up this audit and review.

8.18

It is important that the Government and local agencies take clear steps to address the weaknesses outlined in this report and there is a need for greater oversight and control at all levels. However, the report has also noted that the plethora of guidance and procedures has not always been helpful in enabling practitioners to get on with doing a good job. In moving forward the Government must set clear expectations about the type and quality of services for children it expects to be delivered, and set in place the systems to monitor performance. Both Government and local agencies must consider how best to ensure desired outcomes are achieved without adding to bureaucracy or resource-intensive reporting mechanisms.

Action that can be taken immediately

8.19

Agencies should ensure all staff are familiar with the findings of this review and the areas for change. Opportunities should be provided for staff to consider individually and collectively how practice can be improved. In particular all agencies should ensure that current practices and procedures enable staff, when faced with concerns about a child, to firstly ask of themselves 'what can I do, or my agency do, to help this child?'. This question should be the cornerstone of all agency practice.

Improving inter-agency co-operation and information

8.20

All the agencies working with children are in the process of improving their recording and information systems. These are longer-term projects and are addressed later in the chapter. The review team was particularly concerned that some weaknesses in information systems meant some children who were clearly at risk of being abused or neglected were not identified as such. In particular, the reluctance of many GPs and hospital clinicians to participate in child protection discussions, case conferences and protection planning was a serious cause for concern. There is an urgent need to ensure that crucial information is available to the right staff at the right time.

Recommendation 1: All agencies should review their procedures and processes and put in place measures – to ensure that practitioners have access to the right information at the right time, and in particular to ensure that:

- **Where children present to medical practitioners with an injury or complaint, practitioners must consider what further information is available from their own or other agencies *before they rule out* the possibility of continuing risk.**

- **Where children present to any hospital, there should be in place mechanisms for checking other health records to ensure a pattern of injuries is not being missed.**

- **Where there have been concerns about possible abuse or neglect, schools, police, health service and social work service files should contain a succinct, readily accessible chronology of events or concerns which can be easily referred to should a further incident or concern arise. This chronology should contain information relating to the child and, where known, information relating to other people in the child's life, for example, any previous deaths of children of a mother's new partner.**

- **Courts should ensure bail address suitability checks are undertaken in cases where the alleged offence is against children, or in the case of domestic abuse, where children may be at risk.**

- **Caldicott guardians in Health Boards and Trusts should ensure that health professionals are aware of their responsibilities towards the care and protection of children. In particular they should ensure that where children are at risk of abuse and neglect information is shared promptly with other relevant professionals in line with the General Medical Council and the Scottish Executive guidance on when medical confidentiality can be breached.**

Increasing public confidence

8.21

Members of the public have an important and undeniable part to play in protecting children. They should feel confident in referring any concerns about child abuse and neglect that they may have. But in order to do this, they need clear information about how to access services and what they and the child and family referred can expect to happen. All agencies can contribute to an increased public confidence by making their processes far more transparent and by treating referrers with respect. They should work in partnership with local communities to develop services that local people will feel able to use and that meet the needs identified within that community.

8.22

The police, social work, hearings and courts all have protective duties. In order to carry out these duties properly they should work in partnership with other agencies, with families and with the general public. Protective agencies should be easily accessible, should respect the views of other professionals and be prepared to share and pool resources with other agencies for the benefit of children.

8.23

Social work and the police have statutory responsibilities to protect children, but other services have responsibilities towards children, including those who have extensive and complex needs, howsoever occasioned. There is incontrovertible evidence that the impact of effective health, mental health and educational services can have an enormously beneficial impact upon children who have been abused and neglected. They are also key agencies for the provision of preventative measures.

8.24

Voluntary organisations such as Barnardos, Children 1st and Women's Aid offer protective services that range from preventative, community-based projects to specialised therapeutic projects. The voluntary sector is in a position to identify and respond to areas where more specialised provision is required than can economically be provided by local authorities. They are often trusted by the general public and can act as a bridge between families and statutory agencies.

8.25

Confidential services such as ChildLine and ParentLine should not be seen as 'outside' the system. They help children and families to consider their options, assist with referrals and provide support. They should also work in collaboration with statutory agencies to monitor the level of need for protection and to help with the development of child-centred services. Children and young people themselves are also part of the protective network. It is to friends that victims of abuse first turn and young people should be supported as they, in turn, support their friends.

Recommendation 2: Through the Child Protection Committees all agencies should improve access to help for children who have been abused or neglected by:

- **providing for single page contact information for telephone directories, public phones and the web, which identifies local contact points in health services, local authorities, police services, SCRA and the voluntary sector;**

- **providing for services users and referrers, information about how to access help for children about whom they are worried. This should include information about how and when children and young people will be consulted, what will happen after a referral is made and what and how feedback to people who refer concerns will be provided**

Action over the next three years

Improving practice

8.26

Chapters 2 to 4 provided details of a number of concerning situations and deficiencies in professional practice which were found within the sample of cases audited. In those cases where there was immediate concern the team alerted the agencies and further action has been taken. Summarised throughout the report and at the end of Chapter 5 are features of effective practice observed during the review. Agencies should consider with staff the extent to which their current standards match the best and what action should be taken now and over the coming months to improve performance.

8.27

All children who are at risk of abuse and neglect have a right to:

- services that are accessible;

- a prompt response when they seek help;

- raise a concern only once for professionals to take appropriate action;

- be listened to and their views taken account of when decisions are made;

- an assessment of their needs and the risks they face with action taken to meet need and protect them; and

- help to overcome the impact abuse or neglect has had on their health and development.

8.28

Children, themselves, want to talk about their concerns and get help when they need it but they also want to have some control over what will happen to them and their family if they do. To both protect children and take account of their wishes and needs, there needs to be, as described in this report a 'space for negotiation'. In this space practitioners should discuss with the child and others (parents if appropriate, other family members or professionals) what might be the best way forward and the timescales for taking decisions.

Recommendation 3: The Scottish Executive should, in consultation with service providers, draw up standards of practice that reflect children's rights to be protected and to receive appropriate help. All local authorities, health boards, police services and SCRA should undertake regular audits of practice against these standards and report on them annually to the Scottish Executive and local Child Protection Committees.

Developing the responsibilities of the Child Protection Committees

8.29

The current strengths of Child Protection Committees lie in their role in co-ordinating information exchange, procedures and training. The committees also have considerable experience in multi-agency working and in identifying the needs of the most vulnerable children. Some are already undertaking a quality assurance role, reviewing cases on a regular basis; many are not. Moreover, there is no single agency or structure at local level for assuring the quality of inter-agency work or ensuring that resources are combined effectively on behalf of children who have been abused or neglected. Child Protection Committees are best placed to provide this but require to be strengthened.

8.30

Child Protection Committees also have an important role in the provision of information for the public, parents and carers and in the training of staff or volunteers from a range of agencies which have a role in protecting children. For example, youth groups, sports or cultural associations or other providers such as drug or alcohol services.

8.31

Some Child Protection Committees and voluntary organisations already have considerable experience in this area and some have developed resources for parents (leaflets, information points) to assist then in their parenting role, for instance on feeding and nurturing, the needs of young babies and how to hold them, and on disciplining toddlers and children, without resorting to hitting them. Some committees also undertake promotional activities to raise the levels of awareness within communities and ensure people know where to go to receive help.

8.32

The protection of children is a multi-agency responsibility and its achievement should be integral to the planning of children's services. Child protection (or child safety) committees should be part of and accountable to children's services planning arrangements and work on behalf of all children within a given locality.

Recommendation 4: The Scottish Executive should revise the remit of the Child Protection Committees to include:

- **Annual auditing and reporting, to constituent agencies and to the Scottish Executive, on the quality of agency and inter-agency work.**

- **The provision of information to members of the public, volunteers and other professionals.**

- **Assisting a wider range of organisations to help prevent abuse and neglect through training for staff and volunteers.**

- **The development of safe recruitment practices for agencies working with young people.**

Recommendation 5: Local authority Chief Executives, in consultation with other services, should review the structure, membership and scope of the Child Protection Committee covering their authority and report to their Council and partner agencies on whether it is best constituted to take on the responsibilities for assuring the quality of agency and inter-agency services and the recommendations about their role contained in this report.

Improving learning

8.33

Many of the improvements in child protection have been made following inquiries or reviews of practice when things have gone wrong. This review has provided an opportunity to learn from best practice and to consider what works in protecting children and meeting their needs. To continue to learn and develop knowledge, will require a number of approaches. The final recommendation will result in considerable knowledge about best practice and what works and this will need to be published and shared on a national basis.

8.34

The report has discussed the different approaches to how deaths of children are reviewed both in Scotland and elsewhere. More systematic reviews of all child fatalities would enable greater learning and the development of prevention programmes. It is important that such reviews are established on a statutory footing, they are undertaken by experienced and skilled reviewers and there are mechanisms in place for the dissemination of and learning from the findings at both local and national level.

8.35

Few children who are abused or neglected die or are so seriously injured that they are permanently disabled. Yet many children's lives are blighted through maltreatment and this contributes to later poor educational and work records, offending, drug misuse, mental health problems and poor parenting and further neglect of the next generation of children. We need to know more about long-term effectiveness and outcomes of agency action and intervention. We need to have greater knowledge about what works, as well as what fails and we need to know more about how to improve children's longer-term wellbeing and development following experience of abuse and neglect.

Recommendation 6: The Scottish Executive should consult on how child fatality reviews should be introduced in Scotland. This should include consultation on how they should be conducted, how review teams should be constituted, to whom they would report and what legislative framework is required to ensure their effectiveness.

Recommendation 7: The Scottish Executive should strengthen the current arrangements for the development and dissemination of knowledge about abuse and neglect. In particular it should identify:

- **the most effective arrangements for recording and collating examples of effective practice;**

- **the delivery of staff training across all disciplines or agencies;**

- **the best means of disseminating research findings and best practice; and,**

- **the links between research and knowledge and staff education and training and how this can be consolidated.**

Recommendation 8: The Scottish Executive should initiate a long-term study of the effectiveness of current methods of responding to abuse and neglect. The study should follow children from infancy to adulthood.

Resources

8.36

Effective protection of vulnerable children demands resources, principally of finance and staff with up-to-date professional knowledge and the skills to apply it in a range of practical situations which can be extremely stressful and urgent. Some staff lack relevant training, particularly medical practitioners.

8.37

The lack of resources for children who have been abused and neglected is a matter of great public concern. There are also recruitment problems in health services and social work services. There is a shortage of educational psychologists and the Scottish Children's Reporter's Administration is very stretched.

8.38

Some children live in very poor circumstances and the outcomes for a good number of them will not be improved whilst they remain at home with their families. A number of children are at home because the alternatives – foster care or residential care – are viewed to be either insufficient or of poor quality and in residential care homes they may be at risk from other young people. Other shortages include the lack of help or therapeutic resources for children who are in severe distress or are already severely damaged by their experiences.

8.39

There is clear evidence that some agencies and areas are under considerable pressure. In most local authorities, expenditure on children's services is significantly above the level indicated by the Grant Aided Expenditure (GAE) figure. It is not clear how well resources are being used overall. This report has already noted the high levels of duplication and that resources are often used to meet system requirements rather than meet children's needs. Estimating in specific terms the current financial commitment to child protection is beset with problems. But across statutory agencies the commitment is considerable, not only in direct terms of financing social work Children and Families teams and the Hearing system but in aspects of wider services such as police, education and health. The voluntary organisations such as Barnardos, ChildLine and Women's Aid also contribute significantly with grant support from the Scottish Executive and local authorities.

8.40

The review concluded that as part of improving the protection which children are entitled to expect in a modern civilised society:

- resource priorities need to be aligned to implement the key recommendations;

- they need, at the same time to be increased to overcome obvious deficiencies and gaps; and

- expenditure should be more closely tied to meeting the individual needs of children and their families.

8.41

The Scottish Executive and local agencies are agreed on the principle of moving towards outcome agreements for public expenditure. Increasingly, and most recently in the announcement of the Scottish Budget for 2003-2006, additional funds are tied to clear statements of the expected outcomes. For instance, *Building a Better Scotland* gives a clear priority to outcomes for children and young people: it states,

Objective 1: Closing the opportunity gap by: putting children and young people and their families first; ensuring they are safe and do not threaten the safety of others; promoting equality, inclusion and diversity; and developing values and citizenship.

Target 1: By 2006, ensure that at least 15,000 vulnerable children under 5, every looked after child, every pupil with special educational needs and every child on the child protection register have an integrated package of health care and education support which meets their needs.

8.42

This target, like others, is clearly important in achieving the improvements that this audit and review have confirmed are much needed. Whilst outcome objectives and targets are now driving national *allocation* of resources the targets are unlikely to be realised unless they also drive the *application* of resources at a local level. The Scottish Executive and local authorities have been piloting local outcome agreements as a means of moving towards better focusing the application of resources on outcomes, and lessons can be drawn from these pilots.

Recommendation 9: Children's Services Plans should be developed so that they include clear plans for the implementation of national priorities and demonstrate the application of resources to these outcome targets set out in *Building a Better Scotland.*

Recommendation 10: Local authorities' plans for integrated children's services, as the overarching plans and drivers for all local children's services, should develop *positive childhood* initiatives. These should be lead by a children's rights rather than a public service perspective and should promote <u>every</u> child's rights to life, health, decency and development. The Executive should support this with a public campaign.

Recommendation 11: The Scottish Executive should:

- **advise on how agency resources can be pooled and what systems may best be deployed to ensure the most effective joint commissioning of services on behalf of children; and**

- **commission a study of the costs and benefits of the current child protection system in Scotland and identify costed alternative options for improving outcomes for children.**

Wider problems that relate to child protection

8.43

Whilst agencies are to be commended for recognising that domestic abuse constitutes emotional abuse of children and that children are also at risk of being physically and sexually injured themselves, the response to the problem to date has been haphazard. There is a danger that progress may be undermined if women find that their children are immediately viewed as in need of 'child protection' when they make a complaint to the police about their partner's violence. Current policies of treating every domestic abuse case, where there are children in the home, as a child protection matter or as a matter for immediate referral to the Reporter are not helpful. Agencies and professionals need to exercise greater levels of judgement, in consultation with others, about the best approach to securing a child's welfare, and recognise that protecting the mother may be the best way to protect the child/ren.

8.44

A more comprehensive and unified approach to meeting children's needs should remove the need for automatic referrals to the Reporter of cases of domestic abuse (or any other category of abuse). Providing for the needs of children living in households with domestic abuse should be a priority for inter-agency planning specifically through

- the provision of information for mothers and partners about the impact of domestic abuse on children;

- programmes for reducing its occurrence;

- helping boys and girls develop respectful relationships through the school curriculum and projects such as 'the Healthy Respect' demonstration project in Lothian; and

- ensuring services are available for children who have experienced domestic abuse.

8.45

Agencies tackling domestic abuse need to place more emphasis on working with men to challenge them about their behaviour and to assist them in changing it. Criminal justice social work services have developed a number of approaches to working with men who use violence and the skills and resources that have been developed should be shared with childcare or health colleagues.

8.46

Many children are being abused in different ways and are at risk from a number of people in their lives. Those working with children appear to have most difficulty helping children where there is drug or alcohol misuse, chronic long-standing neglect or domestic abuse.

8.47

The problems of neglect and problem drug or alcohol use are often related, particularly where household finances are spent on drink or drugs or the behaviour of the parents or their associates impact on the child's welfare. Some problems are inter-generational, particularly neglect. The future wellbeing of a large number of children who are now being born into drug misusing families is of serious concern and ensuring their better protection must be a priority. The children's planning frameworks should provide a useful mechanism for tackling these problems at a local strategic level. This would need to be undertaken with Drug and Alcohol Action Teams and Domestic Abuse Multi-Agency Partnerships and take account of the messages in *Getting Our Priorities Right*.

8.48

History tells us that problems of neglect and drug and alcohol problems are associated with poverty and deprivation and that improving the wellbeing of the poorest citizens will make a significant impact. Currently the Scottish Executive is working, alongside the UK Government, to eliminate poverty, improve employment prospects and give children a better start in life. Programmes such as 'Sure Start' and 'Starting Well' which aim to support vulnerable families during a child's early years are providing a valuable preventative resource. Nonetheless there also needs to be a more specifically targeted focus on the most vulnerable children with a concerted effort over the next few years to make a real impact. The review shows that in cases where an early focused approach to tackling the issues is undertaken, change and improvements are possible.

Recommendation 12: There needs to be a new approach to tackling risks and the needs of the most vulnerable. As a first step this should start with assessment of the needs of all new-born babies born to drug or alcohol misusing parents; parents who have a history of neglecting or abusing children and parents where there have been concerns about previous unexplained deaths in infancy. The inter-agency assessment and subsequent action plan in respect of each child should clearly state:

- **standards of child care and developmental milestones the child is expected to experience or achieve;**
- **resources to be provided for the child or to assist the parents in their parenting role; and**
- **monitoring that will be put into place along with contingency plans should the child's needs fail to be met.**

8.49

The approach should be evaluated from the outset and lessons learned about how best to help children at birth and into childhood. It will require the development of systems to identify children who, for whatever reasons, have additional support needs if they are to satisfactorily meet health and social developmental milestones and grow up safely.

Creating greater coherence

8.50

The three main aspects of child protection – protection services, criminal justice and children's hearings – are not well aligned. Professionals should be able to respond to children's needs in a holistic way, in the spirit of The Children (Scotland) Act 1995 within a single coherent system for meeting children's needs.

8.51

The interfaces between children's services and the Hearing systems need to be improved to address the weaknesses identified in this report:

- the combined systems are cumbersome and lengthy;

- some practitioners are using the Hearing system as an alternative route to seeking help for children thus creating more unnecessary work;

- the grounds for a Hearing or the reason for intervention because a child is 'in need' or 'at risk' are not aligned;

- children may remain unprotected because the risks they face do not fit into the categories available;

- children and their parents may be subject to at least two sets of investigations, reports, meetings and decisions and may also be subject to a further set of proof Hearings; and

- there is too much duplication of effort.

8.52

The original principles underpinning the Hearing system have, to some extent, become diluted by the routine referral of particular types of case and by its use as a perceived alternative route to services. Referral to the Reporter should be reserved only for those situations where a person or local authority has cause to believe that compulsory measures of supervision may be necessary.

Recommendation 13: In keeping with the philosophy of the Children (Scotland) Act 1995, agencies referring to the Reporter should indicate what action they or their agency has undertaken to achieve change through consent and why compulsory measures of supervision may now be necessary.

Recommendation 14: The Scottish Executive should review the grounds for referral to the Children's Hearing system. Specifically, it should explore the feasibility of grounds being framed to reflect more clearly the needs of the child and to be more closely aligned with definitions of need outlined in the Children (Scotland) Act 1995.

Improving Information, Assessment, Planning and Recording

8.53

The review has identified a number of inter-related weaknesses in information, assessment, planning and recording systems which can seriously undermine professional practice and which, therefore, need to be resolved as soon as practicable:

- intra-agency weaknesses where practitioners did not have access to information on which to make assessments as the current systems did not allow for timely retrieval;

- inter-agency weaknesses in information exchange and sharing;

- too much duplication of effort with different information kept for different purposes even though the needs of the child remain the same;

- plans in one forum, for example child protection or Looked After Children reviews or Hearings may be different from those agreed in another;

- detailed weaknesses in the clarity and accuracy of records, the relevance of the information and the lack of differentiation between fact, assessment and decisions; and

- the poor quality of information for both practice and accountability.

8.54

A number of these problems have been previously identified and are currently being addressed. But a number still require serious attention.

8.55

Better information and more information sharing are crucial for better management and delivery of services to protect children. Technological developments are already driving improvements in agency recording and information systems. The wider use of information technology presents great opportunities for progress, but it brings with it practical questions about its place in the wider context of personal services and about the sensitive and sensible links it should have with the systems which underpin those services. Planning change in this field requires:

- resolution of the technical problems in getting systems to talk to each other;

- agreement on definitions to be used;

- agreement on co-operation between agencies; and

- definition of the ways of making collective use of social care information for policy and planning and for effective delivery of services.

8.56

The Scottish Executive and other service interests are working to 'join up' these new information systems (through, for instance, the Modernising Government Fund projects) so that agencies can communicate and share information electronically and ensure that all information of common interest about individual children is made quickly available to partner agencies. Access to, and use of, designated areas of information is to be subject to protocols, reflecting the responsibilities and needs of 'subscriber' agencies. This sharing arrangement is to be complemented by information which each organisation holds for its own purposes and which may be transferred to other agencies, as circumstances require.

8.57

The vision is for a number of inter-related systems from which authorised people, by agreement, can extract relevant information. Protecting children should figure as a priority within these systems and should enable, for example, the Reporter to access the current assessment and plan of action for a child, a social worker to access the educational progress of a looked after child and mental health and guidance staff to access a shared area of the information system to up date work being undertaken with a child. It should also enable relevant professionals to have 'real time' access to information about vulnerability or child protection concerns.

8.58

Cumulatively, such developments hold out great advantages for improving child protection:

- rationalising a number of different records and enabling all agencies to contribute relevant information;

- ensuring professionals working to protect children have access to information such as vulnerability factors relevant to their decisions;

- prioritising shared identification and assessment of need, plans for action and the intended outcomes for the child;

- pooling and making information quickly and readily available to all agencies, so that they can respond quickly to changes in needs and circumstances;

- ensuring that medical practitioners and other health professionals provide information to other disciplines in accordance with agreed protocols, for example, through new and closer links with Accident and Emergency information systems;

- providing a clear structure for initiating and maintaining records on vulnerable children; and

- promoting clarity and consistency in the interpretation of rules of professional confidentiality.

8.59

The Scottish Executive is currently developing with social work, education and health interests an inter-agency recording and assessment framework for children. This is a welcome development and should lead to significant practice improvements. To avoid mechanistic application of the framework it will need to be accompanied by extensive training and skills development in its use. It will also need to incorporate standards necessary for effective child protection to:

- be clear, accurate and up to date;

- contain all relevant information including details of concern;

- differentiate between fact, assessment and decision;

- be accessible to all those who need to use it; and

- provide an 'audit trail' to account for decisions and actions taken in relation to children and their families.

Recommendation 15: In order to meet the shortcomings identified in this report, developing linked computer-based information systems should include a single integrated assessment, planning and review report framework for children in need. For those in need of protection the framework should include reason for concern, needs of the child, plans to meet them and protect them when necessary, and progress since any previous meetings. This core assessment, planning and review framework should be accessible and common to all partner agencies, multi-agency case conferences and the children's hearing. Arrangements should be made for appropriate access to information by agencies in other areas should children or their families move.

Developing professional skill

8.60

It is clear that working as a social worker, police officer, health visitor or paediatrician with the most vulnerable children and their families is both highly rewarding and stressful. It is stressful because so much is expected and failure is so well publicised and visible. It is also stressful because, as outlined in this report, the job is not well constructed with its focus on investigation and protection rather than meeting needs, one of which may be for protection. It is an area of practice where much needs to be done and there are significant opportunities for making a real difference. It is also an area of practice where there is considerable evidence of staff commitment, even passion, for the work.

8.61

There is a shortage of skilled staff working with children and their families in local authority settings. Local authority social work is not attractive to many children's social workers who prefer the voluntary sector or special projects which offer the best opportunities to work directly with children and their families. Inevitably then, it is sometimes the most inexperienced staff who are at the firstline of child protection work. Achieving a competent skilled workforce will require action on a number of levels. Scottish Ministers have already agreed:

- significant increased funding for the Reporter service;

- a 12-point Action Plan to address social work and social care workforce issues;

- to increase the number of trainee psychology places; and

- a review of the role and training for guidance teachers.

8.62

The review identified many practitioners who were familiar with research and had up-to-date knowledge of best practice, but were not always putting this knowledge to good effect. There was, across all agencies, an over-reliance on procedures and guidance, sometimes to the detriment of the child. Developing more child-centred informed practice requires confident and competent professionals.

8.63

Increasingly, professional decisions are challenged in the courts. Practitioners must account for their evidence gathering and approach to assessment but also for the underlying reasoning behind conclusions that are reached. This requires a level of knowledge and understanding that is not currently in place. There is a strong need for:

- practitioners working in the field of child care who are experienced;

- methods of diagnosis and assessment that are validated;

- improved evidence gathering and recording;

- clear plans that directly address identified needs and risks;

- mechanisms for monitoring of progress, outcomes; and

- identified thresholds for taking protective action.

Practitioners across all disciplines need to be better informed about what works in child protection and how to implement best practice. At a national level there is a need for more evaluation of practice in order to identify what works. This is especially important in a field where practice developments to date have largely been led by inquiries into what has gone wrong, rather than what has worked for children.

8.64

In order to deliver high quality services practitioners need:

- National outcome standards for protecting children in practice to set the direction for their work (see Recommendation 3).

- Local agency and inter-agency guidance to ensure all staff are supported when undertaking their professional roles.

- To be professionally qualified, experienced and competent in order to make sound professional judgements.

- To have opportunities to continue to improve their skills and knowledge through skills development, access to research and opportunities for learning.

Recommendation 16: The Scottish Executive in partnership with the regulatory bodies should consult on the minimum standards of professional knowledge and competence required of practitioners who undertake investigations, assessments and clinical diagnosis when working with children and their families. In particular it should establish the minimum necessary qualifications and experience required of those making decisions that fundamentally affect the future wellbeing of children.

Proposals for following up this audit and review

8.65

The agenda for change is substantial and will involve a number of agencies. It will need to be progressed at national, agency and practitioner level and it will cut across the work of all agencies working with children. It should be responsive to local circumstances and build on the various programmes and developments that have taken place in recent years. In line with the report's recommendations of a unified system for meeting need, the oversight and management of the programme for change should be located within existing multi-agency structures. At a national level the work would be best located within the current arrangements for taking forward *For Scotland's Children* and a five-year agenda for change with clear outcomes as outlined in this report will be needed.

Recommendation 17: The Scottish Executive should:

- **Establish a national implementation team to take forward the recommendations in the review, in particular the development of standards and local auditing processes.**

- **Establish a review process for annual reporting on progress and improvements.**

- **Implement a further national review of child protection in three years' time to be undertaken by a multi-disciplinary inspection team using this report as a baseline against which progress can be assessed.**

"It's everyone's job to make sure I'm alright."

Appendix A

People involved and consulted during the review

The Review Team

The team was led by Deputy Chief Social Work Services Inspector, Stella Perrott, and the members were:

Jane Bowen – HM Inspectorate of Education

Dr Brigid Daniel – Social Work Services Inspectorate – sconded from Stirling University

Alistair Gaw – Social Work Services Inspectorate

Philip Jackson – seconded from Scottish Children's Reporter Administration

Dr Jacqueline Mok – seconded from Lothian University Hospitals NHS Trust

Jan Ramchurn – seconded from Lothian Primary Care Trust

Ian Ross – HM Inspectorate of Police – seconded from Lothian & Borders Police

Dr Sharon Vincent – Researcher, Social Work Services Inspectorate

The team was assisted by a Co-ordinator (David Purdie) and Assistant Co-ordinators (Jacqui Bow and Teija Campbell)

The Steering Group

Angus Skinner, (Chair) Social Work Services Inspectorate

Dr Ian Bashford, Scottish Executive Health Department

Gerald Byrne, Scottish Executive Justice Department

Margaret Cox, Scottish Children's Reporter Administration

Graham Donaldson, HM Inspectorate of Education

Norma Graham, HM Inspectorate of Constabulary

Lesley Irving, Scottish Executive Justice Department

Jo Knox, Scottish Executive Justice Department

Jackie McRae, Scottish Executive Health Department

Alastair Merrill, Scottish Executive Education Department

Godfrey Robson, Scottish Executive Health Department

Gill Stewart, Scottish Executive Education Department

The Consultative Group

Association of Chief Police Officers

Association of Directors of Education

Association of Directors of Social Work

British Association of Social Workers

British Medical Association (papers only)

ChildLine Scotland

Children 1st

Child Protection Committee Chairs

Children's Panel Chairmen's Group

Commission for Racial Equality

Convention of Scottish Local Authorities

Crown Office (papers only)

Glasgow Centre for the Child and Society

Royal College of Nursing

Scottish Children's Reporter Administration

Scottish Council of Independent Schools

The Law Society

The Safeguarders' Association

Who Cares? Scotland

Scottish Women's Aid

Chairs of the Child Protection Committees

Prof. Norma Baldwin	Dundee City
Safaa Baxter	East Renfrewshire
Chris Booth	North East Scotland
Ewen Cameron	Falkirk
Dr Charles Clark	North Lanarkshire

Brenda Doyle	South Lanarkshire
Brian Fearon	Clackmannanshire
Jimmy Hawthorn	Scottish Borders
Dr Jamie Houston	Argyll and Bute
Iain Macaulay	Comhairle nan Eilean Siar
Peter Macleod	Renfrewshire
Duncan McAulay	Edinburgh and the Lothians
Fred McBride	Stirling
Arthur McCourt	Highland
Gordon McIntosh	Angus
Keith Makin	Dumfries and Galloway
Michelle Miller	Shetland Islands
Ian Mitchell	North Ayrshire
Stephen Moore	East Ayrshire
Robert Murphy	Inverclyde
John Pease	Fife
Gwen Proctor	Perth and Kinross
H Anne Ritchie	West Dunbartonshire
Jackie Robeson	Glasgow City
Jenny Thompson	South Ayrshire
Bill Whyte	East Dunbartonshire
Adrian Williams	Orkney Islands

Formal consultation

The following organisations responded to the consultation exercise:

Aberdeen City Council: Social Work & Community Development Department

Aberdeenshire Council: Education & Recreation Dept

Aberlour Child Care Trust

Association of Chief Police Officers in Scotland

Association of Directors of Social Work

Argyll and Bute Women's Aid

British False Memory Society

British Medical Association Scotland

Central Scotland Child Protection Consortium

Central Scotland Police

Children Are Unbeatable! Alliance

Children in Scotland

City of Edinburgh Council & Edinburgh & Lothians Child Protection Office

Clackmannanshire Council (area response)

Community Child Health Services, Springburn Health Centre, Glasgow

Deaf Blind Scotland

Deaf Society (Edinburgh & East of Scotland)

Dundee City Council & Dundee Committee for Child Protection

Dunfermline Women's Aid

East Dunbartonshire Council

East Dunbartonshire Women's Aid

East Kilbride Women's Aid

East Lothian Women's Aid

ENABLE

F.A.C.T. (Falsely Accused Carers and Teachers)

Falkirk Child Protection Committee

Families Need Fathers Scotland

Fife Acute Hospitals NHS Trust

Fife Council Education Service Child Protection Working Group

Fife NHS Health Board

Fife Primary Care NHS Trust

Forth Valley Primary Care NHS Trust

Glasgow Caledonian University, Dept of Nursing & Community Health

Glasgow Children's Panel

Glasgow Women's Aid

Grampian University Hospitals

Royal Aberdeen Children's Hospital

Grandparents Apart Self Help Group

Greater Glasgow Primary Care NHS Trust

Hamilton & Clydesdale Women's Aid

Headteachers' Association of Scotland

Highland Police, Orkney Area Command

HM Chief Inspector of Fire Services

Inverclyde Women's Aid

Lanarkshire Acute NHS Trust – Monklands Hospital

Lanarkshire NHS Health Board

Lanarkshire Primary Care

Lothian NHS Health Board

Midlothian Child Protection Liaison Group

Midlothian Women's Aid

Moray Council Children's Panel

Moray Women's Aid

Napier University, School of Community Health

National Dental Advisory Committee

NCH Scotland

NHS Greater Glasgow Health Board

North Ayrshire Women's Aid

North Lanarkshire Council, Child Protection Committee

Perth & Kinross Council

Perth & Kinross Child Protection Committee

Perth & Kinross Child Protection Monitoring Group

Renfrewshire Council, Children's Panel Advisory Committee

Renfrewshire Council, Education & Leisure Services

Renfrewshire Council, Social Work Dept

Robert Gordon University, School of Nursing and Midwifery

Royal College of Nursing Scotland

Royal College of Paediatrics and Child Health

Royal College of Physicians and Surgeons of Glasgow

Royal College of Psychiatrists, Child and Adolescent Section

Scottish Borders Child Protection Committee

Scottish Criminal Record Office

Scottish Out of School Care Network

Scottish School Board Association

Scottish Women's Aid, Children's Policy Development Group

SEHD, Scottish Medical and Scientific Advisory Committee

Sense Scotland

Shetland Women's Aid

South Ayrshire Children's Panel

South Ayrshire Women's Aid

South Lanarkshire Council Education Resources

South Lanarkshire Child Protection Committee

Stirling Council

Stirling Royal Infirmary – Paediatric Liaison

The Scottish Institute of Human Relations

University of Aberdeen, Faculty of Education

University of Dundee, Faculty of Medicine, Dentistry and Nursing

University of Edinburgh, Forensic Medicine Section

University of Glasgow, Nursing and Midwifery School

Victim Support Scotland

Volunteer Development Scotland

West Dunbartonshire Council – Education & Cultural Services

West Lothian Council, Community Services

West Lothian Child Protection Interagency Group

Youth Scotland.

Expert consultation

The team consulted a number of organisations and individuals on specific issues which were covered in the review:

Prof Norma Baldwin	Dundee University
Roger Bulloch	Dartington Social Research Unit, Totness, Devon
Dr Sadia Shin Wari Beema Kumari	Council of British Pakistani's forced marriages Incompatible Marriages Project (Scotland)
James C Conroy and Doret Dervyter	University of Glasgow
Pam Cooke	University of Nottingham
Kathryn Goodwin and David Brown	Home Office Research Unit
Jim Ennis	Dundee University
Dr. Elaine Farmer	University of Bristol
Claire Houghton	Women's Aid
Kirstie Maclean	Scottish Institute for Residential Child Care
Ruth Marchant	Triangle
Prof Kathleen Marshall	Independent legal adviser
Prof Helen Roberts	City University/St Bartholomew's Hospital
Nabirye Higenyi	Shakti
Martha Shortreed	Scottish Borders Deaf Children's Society
Prof Olive Stevenson	University of Nottingham
Ruth Stark	BASW
Chief Inspector Lesley Warrander	Lothian and Borders Police
Prof Richard Wellbury	University of Glasgow

Appendix B

International Perspectives on Child Protection

Report of a Seminar held on 20 March 2002

Malcolm Hill, Anne Stafford and Pam Green Lister
Centre for the Child & Society
University of Glasgow

Summary of key issues

Introduction

This report provides an account of a seminar about international perspectives on child protection, held on 20 March 2002. The report presents summaries of the main discussion points and implications.

The seminar was organised by the Centre for the Child & Society on behalf of the Scottish Executive as part of the Executive's review of child protection arrangements in Scotland, *'It's Everyone's Job to Make Sure I'm Alright'*. The review was prompted by an inquiry into the death of 3-year-old Kennedy McFarlane. The aims of the review were to promote the reduction of abuse or neglect of children, and to improve the services for children who experience abuse or neglect. Members of the Scottish Executive and review team attended the seminar, along with individuals from other agencies who belonged to the review's Consultative Group.

The purpose of the seminar was to provide the Child Protection review with information and ideas from other countries to stimulate learning and thinking about how the Scottish system and approach to child protection might be improved. Such comparison would give an opportunity to examine alternative directions and critically re-examine the Scottish situation in the light of the differences and similarities that emerged. One of the speakers invoked a metaphor from a famous Scot, R.D. Laing, that:

'Comparison allows you to unpickle yourself from your place in the pickling jar and see that there is a different kind of life.'

It is possible for specific ideas to transfer productively across national boundaries, as the Family Group Conference has illustrated, but usually some degree of fit is required with the existing values and structures and also some adaptation to them. Probably just as important is that a comparative view helps highlight what is desirable and feasible to change, as well as what is worth retaining and strengthening.

Appendix B

Child abuse and child protection can be defined in very broad terms (National Commission 1996). In order to give the seminar a sharp focus and accord with the priorities of the review, it concentrated on the identification of intra-familial abuse and responses to abuse within the family.

Contributions to the seminar covered other 'Western' countries that are reasonably prosperous and have well established welfare systems, since the transfer of ideas, policies and practices tends to be easier between countries that have similar socio-economic systems. Within that broad common ground, contributors were chosen for their ability to share knowledge about child protection systems that were different from those in Scotland and/or included innovatory approaches. It was decided not to include contributions with a focus on England and Wales or the United States, partly because the bases for child protection in these countries are very similar to that in Scotland and they have been the most important external influences, hitherto. Also many of the easily available publications relate to the UK or USA.

The speakers at the seminar covered two types of country. Firstly, were those which have welfare state heritages akin to those of the UK and US – Australia and Canada.[6] Secondly, details were provided about several continental Western European countries, which have distinctive traditions in relation to social and family policy: Sweden, Belgium, France and Germany (See Esping-Anderson 1990; Hantrais 1995; Hill 1995; Clasen 1999). Two of the papers concentrated on a single country – Australia (Tomison) and Belgium (Marneffe), while the other two made comparative analyses of Canada and Sweden (Khoo, Nygren and Hyvönen) and of France, Germany and England (Cooper).

The rest of this summary of key points summarises the key points made in the plenary presentations. This is followed by a review of the main issues raised in workshop and plenary discussions, which were designed to draw out the points that had most impact on participants and to identify the main lessons for child protection policy and services in Scotland. A brief concluding section highlights the most important messages from the seminar.

Contrasts in overall approach to child protection

We begin with a brief overview of the main similarities and differences among the countries considered at the seminar, then present a brief review of each.

Some oversimplification is inevitable when making broad statements about national systems, let alone groupings of systems. There is often diversity within countries, especially those that are federal or have a high degree of decentralisation. All the countries considered at the seminar had considerable common ground, but the presentations and discussion suggested a major distinction between UK-North American-Australian and continental West European approaches[7] (see Table 1). Each of the speakers indicated how the principles and details of the child protection systems were linked to the wider socio-economic contexts and the

---

[6] These are sometimes described in the comparative social policy literature as 'Anglo-Saxon'
[7] See also Parton 1991; Pringle 1998. West European continental welfare states are sometimes divided into two: the Scandinavian (social democratic) and Bismarckian (corporatist)

nature of the social welfare system. While all countries were affected by the revival of economic liberalism in the 1980s, continental West European states have retained a stronger emphasis on social solidarity and public provision.

Table 2. Differences between British/American and Belgian systems

BROAD TYPE OF SYSTEM	UK-North American-Australian	Continental West European
COUNTRIES COVERED AT THE SEMINAR	Australia, Canada, Scotland, England	Belgium, Sweden, France, Germany
TYPE OF WELFARE STATE	Tendency to residual and selective provision	Tendency to comprehensive and universal provision
PLACE OF CHILD PROTECTION SERVICES	Separated from family support services	Embedded within and normalised by broad child welfare or public health services
TYPE OF CHILD PROTECTION SYSTEM	Legal, bureaucratic, investigative, adversarial	Voluntary, flexible, solution-focused, collaborative
ORIENTATION TO CHILDREN AND FAMILIES	Emphasis on individual children's rights. Professionals' primary responsibility is for the child's welfare	Emphasis on family unity. Professionals usually work with the family as a whole
BASIS OF THE SERVICE	Investigating risk in order to formulate child safety plans	Supportive or therapeutic responses to meeting needs or resolving problems
COVERAGE	Resources are concentrated on families where risks of (re-) abuse are immediate and high	Resources are available to more families at an earlier stage

The papers at the seminar indicated that many of the recent developments in Canada and Australia have paralleled those in the UK and USA. Child abuse inquiries, responding to and fuelling public and political concerns, have promoted a focus on attempts to establish conclusively whether or not allegations are false and to identify the risks associated with abusive situations (Parton et al 1998; Waldfogel 2002; Cooper). The common first language has also facilitated mutual influence. Tomison also points to the influence of economic rationalism. However, some provinces and states have introduced much more standardised risk assessment and case response differentiation mechanisms than in Scotland.

By contrast, Sweden, France and Germany – for all their differences – have evolved more gradually, with a strong emphasis on family support and mediation. Belgium, like its neighbour the Netherlands, introduced major changes in the 1980s with the Confidential Doctor service, which placed at the heart of the system easy access to family treatment. It was noted at the seminar that in Sweden and Belgium child protection is rooted in traditional social policies that seek to provide social assistance and public services on a comprehensive basis. This means that not only can specialist services build on the foundations of universal general provision, but they also draw on a greater measure of goodwill towards representatives of the state than tends to be the case in the UK-North American-Australian systems. Cooper noted that in contrast with France, Germany and the other continental countries, the UK also has fewer or weaker institutions mediating civil society, so that relations between government agencies and the public tend to be more distant or antagonistic.

Among the features of child protection in Canada and Australia described by Tomison and Khoo *et al.* were the following:

- high input into investigation;
- prominent use of risk assessment models;
- detailed agency policies and procedures;
- child protection staff with highly specialist roles and often operating separately from other child welfare services;
- targeting of attention on high risk (strong signal) cases;
- mandatory or expected reporting of abuse; and
- ready use of compulsory orders.

As Marneffe pointed out, most of these characterise British and American systems too. She singled out the following contrasts with the Belgian approach:

Table 4: Contrasts in Welfare State and child protection systems

Countries	UK-American	Belgian
GENERAL WELFARE STATE APPROACH	Residual	Universal
STATE-CITIZEN BASIS	Individualism	Solidarity
VIEW OF CHILD ABUSE	Resulting from individual pathology	Linked to common social and parenting problems
APPROACH TO CHILD ABUSE	Authoritarian and punishment orientated	Helping families
CONTEXT FOR DEALING WITH CONCERNS	Expectation to report cases and deal with families in segregated ways	Confidentiality and health promotion
RESPONSES TO REFERRALS	Investigation and collation of information	Immediate help

She notes, however, that the Belgian approach has been under threat as a result of Belgian governmental responses to the Dutroux case. The inquiry prompted moves towards a risk-avoidance, controlling approach as inquiries have done in the UK. Each of the speakers noted how risk-aversion strategies tend to limit the capacity for early intervention by concentrating effort and resources on 'high-risk' cases.

Hitherto Belgium has had a clear separation of its child protection services from legal frameworks and processes. This linked with an emphasis on confidentiality and was intended to promote confidence in professionals among those needing or seeking help. Also the family therapeutic thrust of the work entails mobilising families' own resources rather than doing things to the family (Marneffe). Likewise in Sweden the service works in solidarity with parents, as part of a well developed system of social welfare offered as a right, voluntarily, and with resources to support families. The threshold for intervention is low, so that any concern elicits an early, preventive response (Khoo et al).

Culturally different understandings: culturally congruent interventions[8]

The presentations amply illustrated the complex ways in which cultural differences between countries imbue approaches to child welfare and child protection. Examples of different cultural understandings between countries and temporal changes in orientation include the lack of a term for child protection in Sweden, the recent inclusion of neglect as a form of abuse in Canada and changes in laws regarding sexual abuse in Belgium. The British and American readiness to sever kin ties and place children for adoption following abuse is alien to French and Swedish viewpoints.

A point crystallised by Cooper and generally accepted was the necessity for interventions to be culturally congruent – i.e. the wholesale importing of lessons from elsewhere would not be feasible. Cooper argues that interventions must be appropriate to the prevailing culture and the system.

However the cultural diversity within countries was also emphasised, indicating that a country's culture should not be understood as homogenous. Illustrations include the more parentalist approach taken by Quebec, with its French traditions, than other parts of Canada, and the different timing and nature of setting up specialist teams for child protection in the Flemish and Walloon parts of Belgium. In recent years, Canadian legislation has provided greater autonomy for Native peoples to organise their children's services in keeping with their beliefs and heritage.

Yet measures have been taken which stress that children have certain universal rights, which can be insisted on. These include the emphasis in law on the child's best interests in all the countries considered. The unconditional Swedish ban on the hitting of children indicates that there no allowance on the basis of differing attitudes is seen as acceptable, although the absence of such legislation in other countries illustrates the variety of views that exist on that point. In the UK concern has been expressed that professionals may be over cautious in

[8] See e.g. Channer and Parton, 1990, Phillips 1995, O'Hagan 2001 for further discussion of these issues

Appendix B

intervening in black and minority ethnic families. The dangers of cultural relativism of this sort might lead to black and minority ethnic children being under protected.

All the countries give some scope for variation according to local needs and influences, but Sweden appeared to have the most decentralised system, with significant powers resting with many small municipalities. In Australia, Belgium and Canada the main level for determining law and policy was at the state, province or community level. Ontario appeared to have the greatest thrust towards standardisation of detailed practice, although this trend has also been present in some Australian states.

Risk assessment

The presentations about Sweden, Belgium and France showed that, although concerns about children's welfare are thoroughly explored, this is done largely as part of broad professional or judicial assessments in dialogue with family members in order to reach a shared view of the appropriate response. Evidence was presented from Belgium to show that the introduction of its confidential health-based system, using systemic assessment and intervention, resulted in a much higher rate of referral than previously, but with a very low failure rate.

In contrast the UK, US, Canadian and Australian systems have, to a greater or lesser extent, adopted some kind of more formalised risk assessment. Cooper refers to the widespread culture in child protection of risk aversion, performance monitoring and quality assessment. Risk assessment has a gate-keeping function by producing definitions and categories, which raise thresholds for intervention. This results in fewer people receiving attention from child protection agencies, which fits well with the residual model of welfare policy.

Accompanied by policies, guides, protocols and working definitions, precise risk assessment tools have been used in North America and Australia with the aim of ensuring judgements about eligibility for services or the need for investigation and intervention are standardised and comprehensive. Tomison and Khoo *et al* show that there are differences in how the systems are employed. In the USA risk assessment is used primarily after a decision has been taken that abuse has taken place. Some Australian states use the model at an earlier stage, as an initial assessment tool by centralised intake centres. In Ontario three tools of risk assessment are used in order to establish eligibility for services.

Tomison identifies the benefits and drawbacks of risk assessment models. Statistical models are considered to be more accurate and less judgemental. They enable decision making to follow logical steps and be more consistent from case to case, team to team. They can help target scarce resources and reduce high caseloads. Thresholds are transparent and they can assist inter-agency working when agencies are working to a common conceptual framework.

One danger is that they can act as a rationale and means of limiting resources. Unless accompanied by family support work, they may mean that early intervention to prevent situations deteriorating is precluded. Risk assessment measures may also be applied inflexibly and result in mechanical decision making. No tool can include all abusive factors nor indicate the precise weighting that a factor or combination of factors can be given in any particular situation. Moreover, the research base for risk factor analysis has a number of weaknesses. Hence this approach needs to be used carefully, following appropriate training and alongside professional judgement.

Having considered several of the broader features and contrasts among the countries considered, we now present a brief overview of each country, summarising the material presented in the seminar plenary papers.

Developments in Australia (Tomison)

The Australian system varies from state to state, but there are many common features. Influences have included a large increase in reporting and hence workloads, a wish to provide more specialist and targeted services and a growing realisation of the extent of inappropriate labelling of cases as child maltreatment. Some states and agencies have adopted policies aiming to work more in partnership with families and to differentiate levels of risk and need. They were influenced in part by the British 'Messages from Research'. (Department of Health 1995). North American risk assessment models have also become popular. Tomison argues that the widespread use of risk assessment in Australia is in part a response to the desire to rationalise and in some instances minimise use of resources.

Several initiatives have been established to create tighter case management, notably central intake systems, differentiated responses and structured risk assessment. Central intake teams were introduced to replace more localised offices in order to reduce differences in practice, standardise responses and minimise the impact of resource issues on decision making. There is evidence of some success, for example enabling departments to target scarce resources to the most dangerous cases. However, the teams have usually experienced increased demands, which need to be planned for and responded to with appropriate resources. Moreover, performance indicators based on recorded levels of child maltreatment may encourage staff to improve the figures by re-defining cases rather than through any change in family functioning.

Often central intake teams use a differentiated response system, which relies on categorising families and then taking action that differs according to the category. A variant of this in Victoria (the Enhanced Client Outcome System) has proved popular with staff and is experienced as less intrusive by families. Like most systems, it is more difficult to implement when families are unco-operative.

Besides altering their case management systems, certain agencies have pioneered new ways of helping families. For instance, the Strengthening Families Model in Victoria provides support to families 'at risk' to prevent them becoming child protection clients. Staff work primarily to build on families' strengths rather than modify their deficiencies and seek to engage families in developing their own solutions. Multi-disciplinary teams have been established to deal with all stages of child protection from investigation to intervention. Despite developments such as this, Tomison admits that the Australian system is still struggling to develop better inter-agency partnerships between professionals and to provide parents, particularly those defined as 'at risk', the support they need to address their problems.

Like other speakers Tomison argues that the investigation-driven child protection responses of the early 1990s will fail without support and other preventative services. American evidence about the effectiveness of early intervention programmes has begun to influence Australian agencies. These are increasingly seen as a cost-effective means of preventing social ills like child maltreatment through promoting social competence and fostering resilience. Whole community projects are also proliferating. These have comprehensive strategies to promote mutual help, participation and volunteering in communities, alongside early intervention programmes.

Child protection in Ontario, Canada (Khoo, Nygren and Hyvönen)

Khoo, Nygren and Hyvönen highlight differences between Ontario in Canada and Sweden, with the former apparently having more similarities to Australia – and Scotland. The principles behind child welfare legislation in Ontario are very similar to those of the Children (Scotland) Act 1995. However, in practice there has tended to be an even more sharp emphasis on 'least intrusive intervention' for the majority of cases and concentrated attention on 'high risk' cases. Much stress is placed on efforts to differentiate cases that need full investigation and to take legal and procedural steps in accordance with detailed protocols. Central to the work is the use of highly structured and standardised risk assessment measures resembling those used in parts of Australia.

Workers have the advantage of clear guidance and standardised ways of acting. The main goals are to determine the extent of harm or dangers to children and to take measures to ensure safety. The image and status of social workers dealing with child protection is low, partly because their investigatory and intervention functions are segregated from positive family service.

A high proportion of children (compared with Sweden) are removed from home. Most are in care under a court order and in many of these cases birth parents' responsibilities and rights have been transferred by means of permanent wardship.

---

[9] This term was new to Britain in the late 1980s

Protecting children in Sweden (Khoo, Nygren and Hyvönen)

In Sweden child protection does not constitute a distinct system, but is embedded in a wider system of child welfare. Indeed there is no equivalent term for 'child protection'[9] and the idea of investigation is alien, replaced by assessment. Social workers in Sweden have relatively high status and a positive image. This both reflects and contributes to good relations with the public in general and, usually, service users. Most staff are experienced and well trained.

Child welfare personnel operate within broad duties under family law, which leaves them considerable discretion. They have a duty to intervene if there are signs that children are showing unfavourable development. Referrals are dealt with by means of the typical methods of engaging with families and formulating social work assessments, without recourse to specific risk assessment models. The orientation contrasts strongly with that in Ontario:

Table 6. Ontario and Sweden compared

Ontario	Sweden
Standardised assessments and actions	Flexible assessments and actions
Assessment is forensic	Assessment is psycho-social
Prime focus is to investigate risk and safety	Prime focus is to understand problems and needs
Emphasis on legal authority and regular use of court orders to secure parental co-operation or alternative care	Emphasis on professional authority and voluntary co-operation with parents
The overriding concern is to achieve change so the child is safer	Building relationships with all family members is crucial

Unlike Canada (and Scotland), the principles and procedures of permanency planning have had little influence in Sweden, especially as regards the stress on use of the law to over-ride parental wishes when this is seen to be in children's long-term interests. The Swedish child welfare philosophy is strongly committed to birth family preservation (except in extreme cases). Practitioners regard foster care arrangements as a positive long-term alternative for children, so that adoption and removal of parental rights are seldom considered as options. Flexibility and patience are seen as preferable to strict time limits for progress. An example of the great lengths taken (and expense incurred) to work with families to keep them together while ensuring appropriate care is the possibility of housing whole families together for four months for assessment.

The Belgian alternative (Marneffe)

The Swedish system is very different from that in Scotland, but in many respects resonates with the situation in the UK before Maria Colwell and permanency planning, but significantly enhanced by high quality staff, a wide range of resources and family support orientation advocated during the 1990s (Department of Health 1995; Canavan et al 2000). The Belgian confidential doctor system, however, has at first sight few resemblances. The principal means of dealing with concerns about children's welfare is not through inter-agency investigations with social work agencies taking a lead role. Instead cases are handled by a multi-disciplinary team led by a medial practitioner. As in Sweden, the aim is to engage with the family as a whole on a voluntary basis, whenever possible. Assessment of harm and risk is not the main priority. Rather systemic family therapy principles and methods are used to help parents acknowledge their problems and responsibilities and to achieve change.

Not only is the Confidential Model distinctive, but its introduction contrasted with both the inquiry-driven nature of British policy change and the gradual evolution in Sweden. During the 1980s the Belgian government took a decision to revolutionise the system of child protection by creating the specialist 'Confidential Doctor' service. Marneffe herself was centrally involved in shaping the new system in Belgium, and is currently Director of one of the multi-disciplinary centres set up for prevention and treatment.

Behind the new system lay the principle of not considering child abuse and neglect to be the act of pathological parents but as having grown out of wider social problems. The new system was also designed to give the quality and respect to service users that all families and individuals should be entitled to receive. This would help minimise stigma and avoid the provision of inferior services for the 'undeserving', so that families are encouraged to approach the team in the knowledge that they will not be reported or blamed. Hence access to the service is free, anonymous, confidential and usually inclusive of both parents. When children refer themselves, then confidentiality is normally maintained unless or until the child wants the parents to be involved.

The system is clearly separated from the police and courts. Professionals are not actively looking for proof of ill-treatment, but assist the family to talk openly about family problems and the consequences for the child, in order to establish a shared plan for improving care and protection of the child. Parents are not required to make a confession, but it is made clear to them that the professionals know abuse has occurred.

The service thus has gained positive connotations for actual and potential clients, in keeping with the generally rights-based approach to welfare provision more generally in Belgium. As in Sweden, the professionals operating the service have public respect. Marneffe argues that parents are usually willing to co-operate, since they are less fearful of being punished or having their children removed than in the UK. Moreover, staff are encouraged to focus on positive change within the family, since separation is not a ready option.

The Confidential Doctor service does not deal with all child abuse cases, however. Just under 10% of abusive parents are considered impossible to cope with, for instance on account of chaotic drug addiction or chronic mental health problems. Marneffe claims that the system quickly identifies those families who will not co-operate or cannot be helped, making it possible to take legal action quickly.

Lessons from other European countries

In the final paper presented, Cooper drew on his experience of comparative research in France, Germany and several other European countries to reflect on the general values and principles that underpin different systems and to draw out possible implications for England and by extension Scotland. He argued that each system is a product of a particular history and context, so that wholesale transposition to another country is unrealistic and undesirable. Rather, it is important to see what might work in the context of the UK or Scotland.

Furthermore, no system is problem-free. In all the countries he and his colleagues studied, they found that child protection work was complex and conflicted. Therefore it is unhelpful to expect any system to be satisfactory for everyone. He argues that effective intervention is only possible if the system is flexible and supportive in relation to the anxieties and conflicts workers face.

He believes three vital and interdependent elements provide a basis for judging how systems do or should operate, namely trust, authority and negotiation. For instance the nature of authority held by key professionals and agencies is linked to the capacity to build and sustain relationships, and develop trust in those relationships. While British and kindred systems have sought certainty of judgement as the main guide to action, other systems allow more time and space for negotiation to reach consensual plans. The French Children's Judges, for example, rarely use their authority to impose measures, but instead develop trust and negotiate outcomes with professionals and families. In contrast to English Family Courts (though with more similarity to Scottish children's Hearings), cases can be considered without full legally admissible evidence. When the French children's judge does make an order, s/he is bound to seek parents' agreement, reflecting the strong emphasis on kinship continuity in French traditions.[10] As in Sweden and Belgium, this happens in a context where removing children is rarely the main option and, partly as a result, parents seem less fearful of the system. Similarly, conflict of viewpoint and interest is regarded as something to be worked with, rather than necessitating separation.

[10] Seen also in the concept of 'simple adoption', whereby adopted children maintain some of their links with the birth family

Cooper argues that the split in England between child protection work and the system of family support, as in Ontario and Australia, makes the process of using authority to build trust and negotiate more difficult. He raises the interesting notion of the need for an alternative negotiated space where conflict can be named, discussed and maybe averted (as happens in France and Belgium). The ability to negotiate depends on trust, i.e. beliefs that the other party has your interests at heart and is acting in good faith.

Interestingly, Cooper has begun testing these ideas with some success in Nottingham in collaboration with the NSPCC. A Multi-agency Consultation Forum for Child Protection has been set up for staff working with high-risk complex cases with a view to providing authoritative but reflective consultation on plans and decisions. It authorises workers to exercise professional judgement in difficult circumstances, with the long-term aim of institutionalising reflective consultation to replace the culture of proceduralism which has dominated social work practice in recent times.

Issues highlighted and discussed by seminar participants

The papers provided much food for thought and provoked widespread interest and discussion among participants. This chapter reviews issues and themes that were raised in the workshops and final plenary discussion. Workshop groups were asked to identify:

- What were the key points that interested them?

- The implications for the work of different professionals and agencies in Scotland.

- What might work in Scotland and what not?

- What changes might be needed in law, policy, services and practice?

The main points were recorded at the time and a summary is presented below, grouped into broader themes. Naturally, many of the issues are interconnected.

How much change is desirable or possible?

People were generally agreed that any alterations in the Scottish child protection system should be compatible with prevailing values and principles. Different views were expressed on whether incremental or radical change is needed. Some saw the current review as an opportunity at least to consider a fundamental transformation. The introduction of the Hearings in Scotland during the early 1970s and the Belgian child protection reforms of the 1980s demonstrated that wholesale innovation can be made. Others suggested that the political and cultural climate was not right for root and branch change.

For some, the Children's Hearings already offer many of the benefits attributed to continental European systems, such as accessibility, informality and flexibility. However, there are tensions and gaps between the Hearings processes and the agency-court systems for dealing with child abuse allegations. Many cases in Scotland still need to go to court for proof and there the adversarial nature of proceedings is very difficult for children and the chances of success are low. There was interest in examining more closely the differences and similarities between Reporters and Children's Judges in France.

The wider social policy and service context

One of the key messages to emerge from speakers, endorsed by participants, was the recognition that child protection was not simply a responsibility of dedicated services. The wider system of welfare and universal provision has a crucial influence on the nature of the child protection system and its capacity to respond to children's families' needs.

Moreover, attempts to change child protection policies and services need to take account of the fact that these are embedded in the broader welfare system and affected by attitudes towards the role of the state. One workshop group suggested a combined agenda of extended universal provision, an improved social inclusion agenda and child protection services developing pro-active engagement with families.

Several seminar participants voiced reservations about the French and Belgian systems, wondering if they glossed over issues of power, gender and race. It was also observed that most Continental European professionals find it hard to understand British anti-discriminatory perspectives. This difference in outlook was apparent in critiques from Scotland of family meetings, since the presence of the abusers (who are mainly men) could place children in very difficult if not impossible positions. Another point made was that by 'dealing' with sexual abuse as a within-family matter, the dangers to children outwith the family might not be attended to.

In various ways, it was noted that systems can be affected by fixed thinking. This was illustrated by the ways in which UK-North American-Australian systems tend to pursue legal and compulsory options, while Continental European professionals tend to assume a voluntary arrangement is usually desirable and possible. In the former, adoption is a possible outcome of child abuse, in the latter it is not. A different kind of observation was that professionals and academics may have different awareness and interpretations of research evidence, especially about the nature and prevalence of sexual abuse.[11]

[11] See e.g. Eldridge 2000; Bolen et al 2000

Appendix B

Resources

The point was made that judgements that a system was not working well could result more from the dearth of support services than from the workings of the system itself. Partly as a result of the long-standing commitment to wide-ranging public services for families in many continental countries, assessment and decisions about families were made easier by the knowledge that suitable services were likely to be available. In Scotland, current shortages and work overloads were mentioned (e.g. with respect to health visitors, Reporters, forensic psychiatric places). Lack of staff was said to have diluted some services, while the channelling of money into special projects had left mainstream services starved.

Family or child orientation

In varied ways, the French, Belgian and Swedish systems all appeared to have as their primary focus the family as a whole or the child within the family. This contrasted with British emphasis on separating the interests of children, women and men in families (also found in Ontario and Australia).

The family orientation in continental Europe was presented positively by some as enabling professionals to engage productively with parents for the sake of children and avoiding as often as possible the need to separate children from their families and communities.

Others expressed concern that the child's interests might be subordinated to parents' rights and wishes. More particularly, it was feared that while agencies sought to work with parents, children could undergo continuing abuse, A linked worry was that family therapy may not address effectively issues of gender and power within families.

Also the presumption in favour of keeping the family together might prolong an unhappy experience in circumstances where in Scotland a child would be placed in a substitute family. It was suggested that for some children living apart from an abusive parent figure, any arrangement to meet that person would be unacceptably distressing. On the other hand, the present Scottish approach may be too rigid when children want the abuse to stop but also to maintain a relationship with the abuser.

It was proposed that children and young people should have more influence on the system. For instance, young people's forums and the availability of a designated person to assist a child could be helpful.

The relationship between judicial and therapeutic systems

Child protection in Australia, Canada and England has been marked by professionals' adherence to detailed legal duties and assessments geared towards potential or actual legal measures. Participants at the seminar saw the Scottish system as having a 'softer' legal approach as a result of the Hearings, which allows for child care issues to be handled without necessarily involving prosecution. Nevertheless concern was expressed that many children do not receive quick or appropriate help when they are involved with the courts, as the majority now are. It was also suggested that all the systems with a strong legal component have low rates of self-referral.

In Belgium and Sweden, the responses to child abuse concerns, except in extreme cases, are largely independent of judicial influences. French children's judges are very much involved in determining what happens, but act in a way that to British eyes may seem more therapeutic than legal.

Discussions took place on whether it is now possible in Scotland to think the unthinkable and not prosecute abusers in child protection cases. One powerful argument in this direction is that prosecution does not achieve the desired results. Children are put through extremely difficult proceedings and rarely see a satisfactory outcome. The length of time waiting for court creates problems and delays therapeutic work. However, non-prosecution would remove the opportunity of public disapproval and sanctions for unacceptable acts.

Space for negotiation

Many were intrigued by Cooper's suggestion that it was crucial to clarify the basis of authority, trust and negotiation on which official child protection is based. Some stated that children's Hearings offered a fruitful setting for such negotiation as a matter of routine. Also attractive was the notion of a 'space for negotiation' on a more selective basis, with workers and families able to go and negotiate with external help when they had reached an impasse or were uncertain what to do. Similarly it would be useful to have access to a multi-agency consultation forum where workers can go and be supported in decision making around complex cases. One suggestion was that space should be created where people can negotiate self-reporting.

Despite the many differences in details, it seemed that Sweden, Belgium, France and Germany all shared the capacity to establish relations of trust with parents and children in order to negotiate agreed action whenever possible. Wide discretion was exercised by judges (France), doctors (Belgium) and social workers (Germany and Sweden) in order to adapt to individual family circumstances. This contrasted with the reliance on standardised procedures in the UK. That was also true in Ontario and Australia with the added dimension of highly formalised categorisations of families.

The quality, image and status of child protection professionals

The presentations had mostly examined the role of social workers as the lead professionals in child protection, except in Belgium and France. Many at the seminar were very struck by the contrast between the poor public image of social work and child protection services in Scotland and Ontario, especially compared to the favourable public regard for social work and child welfare in Sweden, the normalised access to the Confidential Doctor service in Belgium and the approachability and mutuality of French children's judges. A further point was that in the UK professionals experience a blame culture whereas elsewhere it is accepted that no system will prevent all child injuries or deaths, so there is a greater preparedness to accept risks and not to vilify individuals when things go wrong. The Dutroux scandal in Belgium has led the government to introduce changes that may undermine the trust and acceptance that has been built up by the Confidential Doctor centres.

The continuity of employment among Swedish child welfare workers also provided a striking contrast with high staff turnover in Ontario, which echoes the position in Scotland, where low job satisfaction and loss of skilled staff are common. The stability in Sweden presumably reflected greater job satisfaction and in turn was likely to foster confidence in experienced and familiar personnel. Another thought was that staff morale is likely to be better when they are given more autonomy and scope for negotiation.

It was seen as valuable for any citizen and members of families where abuse has occurred to have ready access to non-stigmatising, universal services. This could be via public health practices or school-based. Ideally such provision should be staffed by multi-disciplinary teams. The primary responsibility for children should not be owned by just one professional group. In remote areas of Australia, different professionals of necessity operate from a one-stop base. In a Scottish context, some people wondered if joint funding of child protection services and co-location of different professional groupings would be helpful. It is also necessary to ensure that good links are made between children's and adult services (e.g. in relation to drug misuse).

Community 'ownership' of child welfare and protection

The image of services signified a close connection between public trust of the system and its capacity to engage and then work positively with families. Some argued that it is a priority in Scotland to adapt and publicise the child protection system so that it gains the understanding and respect of the whole community and so that professionals are trusted to act in the interests of families. This requires gaining an active commitment by everyone to the project of child protection and child welfare, as illustrated by the saying *'it takes a whole village to raise a child'*. The public were currently said to have a poor understanding of the Hearings system and the role of Reporters.

A number of people present at the seminar said that the public at large does not value children sufficiently. Also 'the family' is often idealised. Pejorative images of young people can be fostered by the media, as with respect to child prostitution. In Victoria, a public education programme has been developed to try and achieve better general understanding. School prevention programmes in Australia have now moved beyond stranger danger to encompass other forms of danger to children, including within their own families.

Confidentiality, referral and reporting

The Belgian system is premised on confidentiality, as the name of the service shows. It was recognised that this facilitates co-operation with parents, but questions were raised whether this might result in the child's views and interests being compromised.

Confidentiality is also a feature of the German approach. It was observed that confidentiality for young people, as in Germany, empowers them and may encourage more to refer themselves. Some qualms were expressed that adherence to children's wishes in this regard might act against their best interests. Also openness can help deal with problems more readily. The introduction of ChildLine as a confidential helpline service had been resisted at first, but was now widely respected.

Few families in Scotland refer themselves directly on account of abuse. Members of the public were seen as reluctant to intervene in relation to others. Schools and doctor's surgeries were seen as good access points. More children might be helped if child abuse was seen as a non-stigmatising public health issue, as in Belgium. In some parts of Australia, the school is a base for services. New Community Schools in Scotland could offer a similar opportunity.

The presentations indicated that it does not matter much whether reporting is mandatory or not. It is the response to any suspicion of abuse that is crucial.

Assessment and decision making

Some welcomed the idea of standardised risk assessment leading to differentiated responses. This could be seen as a form of triage, allowing practitioners to concentrate their efforts on the most needy. On the other hand, evidence from Australia and Canada indicates this may work poorly when it becomes largely an administrative measure. Warnings were also made about the danger that risk assessment schedules would take up a lot of staff time and lead to a more rigid response to families. Their use is also dependent on appropriate training.

More joint assessment extending beyond social work and the police could lead on to better shared understandings. Joint teams in the same location could work together effectively, though there would be a danger of becoming cut off from mainstream services. There is also a need to engage services whose primary orientation is towards adults (e.g. in relation to drug misuse, criminal justice).

Questions were asked about the checks and balances required in any system. Do the French judge and Belgian doctor perhaps have too much freedom to decide and act alone? Similarly, it seemed that social workers in Canada could operate without much external restraint.

Voluntarism versus compulsion

The idea of moving towards a system based more on voluntary agreement and partnership was attractive, but some discomfort was felt too. It was suggested that attitudes about criminality in relation to child abuse may change, as has happened with respect to abortion. Without fear of prosecution or other sanctions, some adults would be more willing to admit that they had ill treated a child and work towards change. On the other hand, might parents become too powerful in the process at the expense of children?

Removal of children from home

In the UK, inquiries, policies and practice have fluctuated in their emphasis on birth family preservation or continuity as a crucial component of children's interests and on the removal of children as a requisite for the safety and development of some children (Harding 1991). Nevertheless, in Scotland as in other UK-North American-Australian systems emergency removal remains a major if reluctant option in investigations, with adoption or permanent fostering regarded as the preferred choice for a small but significant minority of abused children. Knowledge of this has helped shape not only the anxieties of those undergoing investigation, but also the suspicious attitudes of many families in need and the public more generally.

At the seminar people were interested to learn that this is not a feature in all systems. In some European models the possibility of permanently placing a child in another family against parental wishes is barely considered and is anathema in some eyes. Presenters argued that when service providers have no alternative, they are more likely to find ways of achieving a satisfactory solution with the child's birth family. A further benefit is that families are much less fearful of professionals. Even where it seems impossible to work with the families, a 'clean break' is not espoused since the family is seen as a constant in a child's life.

Screening and unresponsive families

There was interest in the fact that across all the different types of systems, seemingly regardless of the approach, a relatively constant proportion of referred cases of between 7% and 10% proved very difficult or impossible to work. Although continental systems are usually more measured in their response than in the UK, it seemed that in Belgium at any rate a quick decision is made when families cannot be helped and alternative, usually court-based, action is needed. This ability to distinguish such families promptly would be useful in Scotland, where such cases may tie up a disproportionate amount of agency time unproductively. Canadian and Australian models do have a screening approach, but based on risk to the child more than prospects of working effectively with the family, although these two will often be related. Another matter to be addressed is the impetus in UK-North American-Australian systems to take action too slowly in some cases and too precipitously in others.

Prevention

Ideas about early intervention were generally welcome. The importance was registered of educating the next generation of parents so they are less liable to ill-treat children.

Domestic abuse

The effects on children of domestic abuse towards their mothers has received growing attention in Scotland. Reporters have experienced an upsurge in this kind of referral, as apparently have French children's judges. Uncertainty was voiced about whether this helps children. Questions were raised about whether family therapy models are appropriate or not. In particular, the emphasis on obtaining family agreement for decisions and actions could mean that parents' power and children's relative powerlessness produced outcomes not in children's interests. In Australia, school-based prevention programmes could be helpful, but the government's wish to portray the family as preponderantly benign may mean that attention to violence within the family is minimal.

Evidence-based policy

The seminar reinforced for some people the importance of having sound evidence, including comparative evidence. However, it is difficult to draw conclusions from national differences, since these can be caused by a wide range of factors. It was noted that broad indicators of children's well-being tend to reflect standard of living and levels of general welfare provision, rather than the specifics of child protection systems. Thus, both Sweden and Canada have very good records in this respect, even though the approach to child protection is very different.

Cooper observed that ideas about child welfare systems are culturally specific, so it is difficult to reach agreement about how to judge outcomes and is more useful to consider principles. The presentations emphasised the value of understanding differences and similarities in daily practice and the assumptions, often taken for granted, that underpin practice in different countries.

Several participants wondered if presenters were talking about the same kinds of family and levels of difficulty or risk, when describing different types of response. It was also unclear how far the apparent success of continental systems in facilitating co-operation in the majority of families was accompanied by a failure to gain a purchase with tough cases. Conversely, the UK-North American-Australian investigative approach may discourage openness generally, but use of the law may help some children where otherwise family closure would leave children unprotected from harm. Set against this is evidence from Australia and Scotland that authorities can be rendered powerless by the insufficiency of legally admissable evidence, whereas continental European professionals or children's judges have the authority to proceed.

Research can guide more specific developments. For instance, evaluations have shown the value of intensive home visiting, yet in Scotland the health visiting service is currently being cut back.

Several participants were conscious of significant gaps in the information routinely available in Scotland to guide policy-making and provide feedback about the operation of the system. There was interest in the idea of a 'Clearing House' along the lines of the Australian one outlined by Tomison. Funded by the federal government, it has an information, advisory, support and research role. There was interest in exploring the possibility of something similar for Scotland.

Conclusions

The aims and length of the seminar were not intended to create consensus about a way ahead for Scotland, but rather to stimulate thinking about possibilities for change. Hence this concluding section of the report does not provide a blueprint for action, but highlights some of the issues that apparently had a strong impact on most participants or that evoked divided responses.

In one way it can be seen as reassuring that all of the systems were grappling with similar issues and none was free of problems or dissatisfactions. In particular, everywhere it is difficult to cater for those families with little capacity to change.

Each of the papers contained details about innovations that might be adapted to the Scottish context, but there was broad support for the view that the most important thing is to be clear about the values and principles that should underpin services in Scotland dealing with child abuse and neglect. Also it was accepted that cultural differences shape welfare systems in various ways, reflecting different values and perceptions as regards child-family and family-state relations, so that grafting ideas from elsewhere needs to be done when they can adapt to the local context and vice versa. 'Bolting on' isolated developments may have limited success. Similarly, the capacity of specific child protection or child welfare measures to achieve change is limited unless they rest on a foundation of good universal services.

Equally it is important to examine or re-examine prevailing assumptions that affect choices and decisions. In several European countries, plans and actions may be seen as either restricted or liberated by the fact that court action is seen as a rare option and that domestic adoption of older children against parental wishes is virtually unheard of. Conversely, professionals in Scotland may be diverted from offering help or working towards voluntary solutions with parents, because of the emphasis on legal solutions.

Allowing for these cautionary comments, two contrasting directions appear possible.

The more fundamental one would be to align the system more with continental West European practices. Key features would include:

- a range of flexible preventive and therapeutic resources;

- an agency, profession or multi-disciplinary team taking the lead role in responding to concerns about children, This requires well qualified staff acting with flexible discretion and trusted by the public, service users and government;

- ready access by children and parents, as well as professionals, to the lead agency sited in a non-stigmatising context, ideally linked and identified with universal services;

- an emphasis on thorough assessment of problems and needs as well as risk, rather than investigation;

- therapeutic help offered quickly without the need to worry about forensic and evidential considerations;

- the goal of achieving solutions agreed with parents and children on a voluntary basis wherever possible;

- resort to the use of courts in only a small minority of cases, but with early identification of those families where this route is necessary; and

- allowing children's wishes about confidentiality and contact with abusing family figures to have a major influence on the timing and nature of communication and decisions.

For the most part, the feedback at the seminar on these qualities of continental systems and their impact was positive. Many of them run against the grain of British social policies, state-citizen relations and judicial traditions, but the Scottish children's Hearings system offers both a precedent for change and a value base that is more consistent with the above elements than the current thrust of central government, local government and court policies and practices. Legal requirements would have to be loosened for professional/judicial autonomy to operate as it does in Sweden, Belgium and France. The requirement to place more trust in achieving voluntary solutions with parents is appealing, but in the context of serious abuse is contrary to trends in the UK. These have moved away from a stress on family unity and optimism about change towards an emphasis on children's separate rights and confidence in the appropriateness of one parent or alternative families meeting their needs. Likewise the British propensity to consider separation when there is persistent violence towards children or women and preparedness to consider long-term compulsory 'clean breaks' would need considerable modification to accommodate a view that children's best interests are almost always located within persisting family relationships, even when these have been negative and disruptive.

Evidence about Ontario and Australia indicate an alternative direction, which involves refinement and standardisation of case and risk management. This would probably entail a less substantial adaptation of the present procedures and mechanisms for handling child abuse in Scotland. Among the key elements might be:

- specialised and possibly centralised intake systems;

- clear categorisation of families so that different kinds and levels of service are provided according to need and risk;

- better targeting of resources;

- more co-operative relationships with families where risk is not high;

- greater consistency of response; and

- emphasis on the child's safety as the primary consideration.

On the whole the presenters indicated more disadvantages than advantages in this approach, especially within a context of limited support services. However, there were also indications that as part of an overall strategy with a strong preventative component, developments along these lines can help overcome pervasiveness of suspicion and compulsion, while retaining the capacity to safeguard the care of children in extreme circumstances with unresponsive parents.

In all the countries considered, evidence indicated the importance of having a child protection service staffed by skilled, experienced people with high public status. Where this occurs in parts of Europe, it is associated with a willingness of society and the authorities to trust in professional judgement. Moreover, in Sweden staff turnover is low and job satisfaction reasonable, whereas in much of Scotland there is low morale and high staff turnover (as in Australia and Canada). These points suggest that attention and resources must be committed to professional education and public information.

In every presentation, the drawbacks were pointed out of having child protection arrangements too closely aligned with judicial processes and segregated from broader child welfare, family support or health promotion systems. Continuity with universal services fosters co-operation and reduces stigma. Yet all systems use compulsion for a minority of extreme cases.

It is important to clarify the relative balance among needs, risks and rights. Each system attempts to meet children's needs, protect children from harm, solve family problems and support parents, but they have different emphases and thresholds for making safety the over-riding consideration. In both continental Europe and parts of Australia, as well as elsewhere, a recent shift has been to work wherever possible with family strengths rather than deficits.

Certain specific ideas were attractive to many participants. The notion of creating space and time for negotiation is useful. Professionals are likely to welcome the opportunity to have time and access to external people in order to discuss their concerns informally. This could be particularly applicable when they are uncertain or the risks not great, without or before invoking the full child protection procedures.

In Scotland, as elsewhere in the UK, a recurrent problem has been the difficulty of giving children effective therapeutic help, because of the way action has been driven by the need to gather evidence for courts. This has often added to children's distress rather than alleviated it (Roberts and Taylor 1993; Westcott and Davies 1996). The Belgian Confidential Doctor system makes very early access to help possible, though some would not wish to import the emphasis on including abusive parents. In different ways, other systems as in Germany appear able to let (older) children's wishes guide communication and action. It would also be beneficial in Scotland to extend the multi-agency co-operation that has been established with respect to investigation into joint or collaborative therapeutic work, as in Belgium and parts of Australia. Whole community preventive strategies are consistent with current social inclusion initiatives in Scotland.

Another valuable measure would be the capacity to identify quickly families who are very unlikely to respond to change efforts. In this respect the prompt assessments made by Confidential Doctor teams produced outcomes that are aspired to by the risk assessment and differentiated response mechanisms used in Ontario and parts of Australia, even though its orientation is otherwise quite different.

A number of issues evoked complex responses and require further thought and discussion. This applied particularly to confidentiality and power relationships.

Evidently plans for any changes in Scotland should be based on thorough assessment of the strengths and weaknesses of the present child protection system, as has been carried out by other elements of the Child Protection review. The seminar showed that there are alternative values, principals, ways of staffing and organising services and specific mechanisms that could help improve arrangements to promote children's welfare and safety in Scotland.

Appendix C

Child Protection in Scotland

UN Convention on the Rights of the Child

In 1991, the UK ratified the United Nations Convention on the Rights of the Child, which has had a significant impact on Scottish law and practice. The passing of the Human Rights Act 1998 made the European Convention on Human Rights a part of Scottish law. This has positive implications for children who are as entitled as adults to benefit from its provisions. The principles of both conventions shaped the Children (Scotland) Act 1995, which is discussed below.

The Convention on the Rights of the Child's explicit focus on children means that it has more obvious implications for child protection. Ratification means that all practice should be shaped by it unless this is actually contrary to Scottish, or European human rights law. Much remains to be done in moving towards full implementation, but we should not underestimate what has been achieved. Statutory and voluntary agencies in Scotland have been active in promoting the convention and continue to work towards greater recognition of it. The convention's particular relevance for child protection lies in its commitment to:

- support for family life;

- respect for the child's views;

- provision of an adequate standard of living, education and health services, to leisure and to a cultural and spiritual life;

- making the child's best interests a primary consideration for Scottish society;

- prevention of abuse and neglect;

- protection from harm;

- help to recover from abuse; and

- identification and investigation of concerns about child abuse and neglect, and follow-up, including involvement of the courts where appropriate.

Scottish legal framework

The Scottish legal framework in relation to child protection centres on:

- Scottish and UK Acts of Parliament, in particular the Children (Scotland) Act 1995;

- rules and regulations made under powers delegated by these Acts;

- principles derived from decided cases; and

- the European Convention on Human Rights, which acts either as a lens through which the above must be interpreted or, in some cases, an immediate corrective where the law does not meet the requirements of the Convention.

The UN Convention on the Rights of the Child is not an integral part of Scottish law in the same way as the European Convention; however, following the practice of the European Court on Human Rights, it should be taken into account when interpreting the European Convention. Scottish courts have also increasingly referred to the UN Convention when considering matters relating to children.

The Children (Scotland) Act 1995 defines and regulates family relationships and sets out the powers and duties of local authorities and other agencies regarding child welfare and protection. Local authorities must collaborate with other agencies to plan and publicise services promoting the welfare of children. They have a duty to safeguard and promote the welfare of children 'in need' in their area by providing services for them or their families. The main aim is to help families stay together. Children are 'in need' if one or more of the following conditions is satisfied:

- they need local authority services to help them achieve or maintain a reasonable standard of health or development;

- their health or development will be significantly impaired if such services are not provided;

- they are disabled; or

- they are affected adversely by the disability of any other person in their family.

Sometimes, family support is not enough to protect children from abuse and neglect. The Act sets out procedures for concerns about child welfare and protection to be passed to the Children's Reporter who will decide whether to refer the matter to the children's hearing (this is discussed later). There are also procedures for obtaining court orders to make sure that children can be seen, assessed and protected where necessary, sometimes through removal from their homes. However, it is a principle of the Act that no court or children's hearing should make an order relating to a child unless it can be shown that this will be better for the child than not making an order.

The legal framework assumes that the majority of parents will act in the best interests of their children. Where they cannot do so, the state prefers to help than intervene. However, support is not always enough. Further, in a small number of cases, the circumstances may be so clear or so detrimental that support is not appropriate. If children are to be protected there must be, and there are, threshold conditions and procedures for compulsory intervention.

Guidance

The legal framework is underpinned by legal regulations and guidance. The guidance to the Children (Scotland) Act provides guidance on the circumstances that might indicate a child is in need, the type of services that might be provided and the key elements for planning services as well as considering the needs of children with a disability or those who need protection.

There are two sets of national child protection guidance in Scotland – national guidelines for all agencies on inter-agency co-operation and specific guidelines for health professionals based on these. There is also a circular for education departments (Circular 10/90), issued in 1990. There are 15 sets of local inter-agency guidance (agencies in the former Strathclyde Region have a common set as do agencies which formed the former Lothian Region, Central Region and Grampian) that seek to apply national guidance locally. There is also separate local single agency guidance: for education, health, police and social work. Up to four different sets of guidance might apply at any one time (national, local inter-agency, area agency (e.g. consortium of Health Trusts), and individual agency/department.

How agencies respond to allegations of abuse and neglect

Pre-referral

Concerns about a child may be expressed by many different individuals – a child's friend; a parent or other family member; a neighbour or other member of the public; a professional or other concerned person (e.g. teacher, social worker, doctor, youth worker, etc.). A child or young person may have told any of these people that they are being abused or neglected, or these adults may have suspected or guessed that something is wrong. Some adults may decide not to tell anyone else about their concerns. Alternatively they may seek advice. For example, it is common for health visitors to keep a list of children about whom they have concerns and they may decide that it is sufficient to monitor a child on the list more closely or they may seek informal advice without making a formal child protection referral about a child. Other people, particularly children themselves, their friends and relatives, but also members of the public and occasionally even professionals, may ring a helpline such as ChildLine or ParentLine Scotland in order to obtain advice about what to do or to talk about their concerns.

Sometimes agencies or other adults may have concerns for a parent rather than a child. For example, a parent may have alcohol or drug problems, financial worries or health problems. In these cases help from social work, or other health services may be sought for the parent so that they can continue to care for their children. In these cases the child may be considered to be 'in need', but not in need of 'care and/or protection'.

Local authorities have a duty to provide services for 'children in need'. They also have a duty to safeguard and promote the welfare of children who are in need and to promote the upbringing of children by their families (so far as this is consistent with promoting a child's welfare.) Assistance might range from the provision of information through support for a family to a residential placement for a child away from home. In most cases help will be provided on a voluntary basis by a social work department in consultation with or in partnership with other departments or agencies.

Referrals

Concerned individuals, having decided that protective action is needed, may refer a case to the social work department, or the police, as the agencies which have statutory responsibility to investigate or make enquiries about child abuse or neglect. Alternatively they may choose to talk to a teacher, doctor or other professional who will make a decision whether or not to make a referral. A referral may also come directly from the child. As well as or instead of contacting police and/or social work, an individual may make a referral to the Reporter. Anyone who has reasonable cause to believe that a child may need compulsory measures of supervision – an individual, agency or court – can make a referral to the children's Reporter.

Investigation

Local authorities have a duty to make enquiries about the circumstances of children referred to them in order to determine if they are in need, if compulsory measures of supervision may be necessary or if a child protection or an exclusion order is needed for their protection. They will also need to make enquiries in order to complete an assessment of need.

The police have a duty to investigate any alleged criminal offences reported to them. Not all incidents of abuse and neglect will be considered to be a criminal offence. The police are involved less frequently in cases of neglect and may not be involved in minor cases of physical abuse. In order to ensure that children are not subject to two sets of interviews and enquiries, police and social work determine which agency should undertake the enquiries or whether a joint approach is needed.

When the social work department or police receive a referral they may decide not to investigate, in which case they will either close the case or decide that the child is 'in need' and provide services to support the family and/or the child. If the referral is serious enough to warrant action as a child protection matter they will undertake an inter-agency investigation in partnership with other relevant agencies or make further enquiries.

Following a joint investigation there should be a joint decision about what further action will be taken. It may be decided that no further action under child protection proceedings is required and the case may either be closed or family support offered. If further action to protect the child is needed, a case conference will be called and also a referral may be made to the children's Reporter.

In some cases it may be necessary to take urgent action, before a case conference or children's Hearing can be called, to protect a child from immediate harm. A child's parents may agree that a child should be looked after by the local authority or by a relative or other member of their social network whilst agencies carry out their investigations. In other cases, agencies may need to take legal action to remove a child from the source of danger by applying for a Child Protection Order. Alternatively, the local authority may apply for an Exclusion Order, which requires the removal of a person suspected of harming a child from the family home. In an emergency and prior to a court Hearing, a police constable may remove a child to a place of safety if he or she considers the grounds for a Child Protection Order are satisfied.

Where a referral is made to the Reporter he or she is required to undertake an initial investigation. The Reporter may request a report from the local authority on any issue he or she thinks relevant and the local authority must provide this report. Reports are likely to be requested from social workers and/or the child's school. Information may also be requested from health, the police, voluntary agencies, Procurator Fiscal, courts, residential units and families. Only if the Reporter considers that the grounds for referral can be proven in court and that there is a need for compulsory measures of supervision will he or she call a children's Hearing. The Reporter must also be satisfied that legal intervention in a family's life, i.e. making a supervision order, is preferable to not making an order. If the Reporter considers that these conditions are met, he or she will call a Hearing. If the Reporter decides that intervention is not possible or not required, for example, if there is insufficient evidence, there will not be a Hearing and there will be no further action. Alternatively a Reporter may decide that intervention is necessary but that compulsory measures are not required in which case he or she will refer the case to the local authority for voluntary assistance. In just under half the cases referred, the Reporter makes a decision that there are insufficient grounds or that formal procedures are not required.

Case conference

A child protection case conference will be attended by relevant professionals, parents and/or other carers, and children and young people where appropriate. The conference members assess the degree of existing and likely future risk to the child. They also assess the child's needs and identify any services that may be required to meet them. The conference may decide that the child's name does not need to be placed on the child protection register and the case will either be closed or family support will continue. Where it is agreed that a child's name should be placed on the child protection register, a child protection plan will be formulated which will outline how the child's needs can be met by all the various agencies. A decision will also be made at the case conference about whether or not to make a referral to the children's Reporter.

Where the parents or carers are refusing to allow social workers to see the child in order to assess risks and needs, a local authority may apply for a Child Assessment Order. An Assessment order requires the parents to produce the child and to allow an assessment to take place.

Review case conference

A child's name will stay on the child protection register until professionals decide that the risk to the child has been sufficiently reduced. Child protection plans have to be reviewed at least every six months. The decision to remove a child's name from the register will be made at a review child protection case conference. If a child's name is removed, the social work case will either be closed or it will be decided that family support should continue.

Voluntary support

Agencies provide services for children directly and services to help parents in their parenting role. Additional help might also be provided to enable parents to overcome personal problems such as drug misuse. Many parents accept such help, but some parents cannot or will not or they continue to be unable to prioritise their children's needs. In these cases the offer or the provision of voluntary support may not be effective and agencies may refer children to the Reporter if they consider that compulsory measures of supervision are needed.

Children's Hearings

Children's Hearings are made up of volunteer lay members drawn from a local 'Children's Panel'. The child and other 'relevant persons' including parents can also attend and may be required to attend a Hearing. A safeguarder may be appointed by the Hearing. The safeguarder will consider the interests of the child to assist panel members decision making. If a child or his or her parents do not accept the 'grounds', or reasons for calling the Hearing, the Reporter will make an application to the sheriff for a finding as to whether the grounds of referral are 'established'. Alternatively, the Hearing may discharge the referral completely.

The same options apply where the child is considered to be incapable of understanding the grounds by reason of age or understanding. Where a sheriff decides that the grounds of referral are established the case will return to the Hearing for a decision. In approximately 80% of 'care and protection' cases, the matter is referred to the sheriff.

Where the grounds for referral are accepted or where the grounds have been established before the sheriff, the children's Hearing will make a decision. It may discharge the referral or, where the Hearing feels the child needs compulsory supervision, it can make a 'supervision requirement'. Although the Hearing's powers focus on considering the need for compulsory orders, their ethos and training encourages the negotiation of consensus between families and professionals and of commitment to work together in the child's interest.

Parents and children can appeal to the sheriff against any decision of a Children's Hearing. Further appeals to the Sheriff Principal or the Court of Session can also be made.

Supervision requirement

A supervision requirement places the child under the supervision of the local authority but in practice it is usually implemented by the social work service. Supervision can include supervision at home, with a relative, in foster care, in residential care or in secure accommodation. A supervision requirement may require a child to reside at a particular place or can give authority for a person to act to restrict a child's liberty. The Hearing may impose any condition about the child to the supervision requirement it sees fit, for example, there may be a requirement that a child receives medical treatment. In addition the Hearing may regulate contact with any person. Unless reviewed and continued or varied, a supervision requirement will not last longer than a year. The Hearing, when reviewing the case, may order a further investigation into the child's situation, terminate or vary the requirement, impose further conditions or simply continue the order without variation.

A child or relevant person may appeal to a sheriff against the decision of a Hearing. The sheriff may appoint a safeguarder to look after the child's interests.

Criminal justice routes

A criminal investigation may be carried out as part of, or in parallel with, child protection enquiries and children's hearings proceedings. The police have a duty to protect the public and to investigate on behalf of the Procurator Fiscal where they believe that a criminal offence may have been committed. Following a joint investigation, the police will send reports of suspected crimes to the Procurator Fiscal. He or she will decide whether criminal proceedings are in the public interest. Public interest includes, but is not restricted to, the interests of children as witnesses or accused. The Procurator Fiscal will take account of Article 3 of the United Nations Convention on the Rights of the Child, to ensure the best interest of the child shall be a primary consideration. He or she may decide that there is a lack of sufficient evidence or there are no grounds for a prosecution. If a Procurator Fiscal decides that it is in the public interest to prosecute then the case will proceed to court.

Appendix D

References

Bolen, R.M., Russell, D.E.H. and Scannapieco, M. (2000). 'Child sexual abuse prevalence. A review and re-analysis of relevant studies', in Itzin, C. (ed.) 2000, *Home truths about sexual abuse influencing policy and practice. A Reader.* London: Routledge.

Brandon, M. *et al* (1999) Learning how to make children safe: an analysis for the Welsh Office of serious child abuse cases in Wales, University of East Anglia/Welsh Office.

Canavan, J., Dolan, P. and Pinkerton, J. (2000). *Family Support: Direction from Diversity.* London: Jessica Kingsley.

Cawson, P. *et al* (2000) Child Maltreatment in the United Kingdom, a study of the prevalence of child abuse and neglect, NSPCC.

Cawson, P (2002) Child Maltreatment in the family, the evidence of a national sample of young people, NSPCC.

Channer, Y. and Parton, N. (1990). 'Racism, cultural relativism and child protection', in the 'Violence against children study group' *Taking child abuse seriously,* London: Unwin Hyman.

Clasen, J. (ed.) (1999) *Comparative Social Policy,* Oxford, Blackwell.

Cleaver, H. and Freeman, P. (1996) Suspected child abuse and neglect: are parents views important? in Platt, D. and Shemmings, D. (eds) Making enquiries into alleged child abuse and neglect: partnership with families, John Wiley and Sons.

Department of Health (1991) Child abuse: a study of inquiry reports 1980-1989, HMSO.

Department of Health (1995) Child Protection Messages from Research, HMSO

Eldridge, H. 2000. 'Patterns of sex offending and strategies for effective assessment and intervention', in Itzin, C. (ed.) (2000), *Home truths about sexual abuse influencing policy and practice. A reader.* London: Routledge.

Esping-Andersen, G. (1990). *The Three Worlds of Welfare Capitalism.* Princeton (New Jersey): Princeton University Press.

Farmer, E. and Owen, M. (1995) Child Protection Practice: Private risks and public remedies - decision making, intervention and outcome in child protection work, HMSO.

Goodman, G.S; *et al* (1992) Testifying in criminal court: emotional effects on child sexual assault victims; Monographs of the society for research in child development, 229, 57,5.

Gray, S. *et al* (1997) 'User centred responses to child sexual abuse: the way forward?' Child and Family Social Work 2 49-57.

Green, L and Mason, H. (2002) Adolescents who sexually abuse and residential accommodation: issues of risk and vulnerability, *British Journal of Social Work,* 32, 149-168.

Greenland, C. (1986). Inquiries into child abuse and neglect (C.A.N) deaths in the United Kingdom, Extract from the *British Journal of Criminology,* Delinquency and deviant social behaviour, 26, 2 April.

Grubin (1998) Sex offending against children : understanding the risk; Police research series paper 99; Home Office Policing and Reducing Crime Unit, Research, Development and Statistics Division.

Hantrais, L. (1994). 'Family policy in Europe' in Page, R. and Baldock, J. (eds.) *Social Policy Review.* Canterbury: Social Policy Assn.

Hamilton, C. and Browne, K.D (1999) Recurrent maltreatment during childhood: a survey of referrals to police, Child Protection Units in England, Home Office Research Development and Statistics Directorate.

Harding, L.F. (1991). *Perspectives in Child Care Policy.* London: Longman.

Health, Department of. {1995). *Child Protection: Messages from Research.* London: HMSO.

Hill, M. (1995). 'Family Policies in Western Europe' in Hill, M., Kirk, R. and Part, D. (eds.) *Supporting Families.* HMSO: Edinburgh.

Hill, M. (1990) The manifest and latent lessons of child abuse inquiries, *British Journal of Social Work,* 20, 197-213.

Hobbs, G. and Hobbs, C. (1999) 'Abuse of children in foster and residential care' *Child Abuse and Neglect* 23 (12) 1239-1252.

Horwarth, J. (2002) Maintaining a focus on the child? First impressions of the framework for the assessment of children in need and their families in cases of child neglect' Child Abuse Review, 11, 4, 195-213.

Ibbetson, K. (1996) Neglect: Learning the lessons of a UK inquiry. Neglect – a fifty year search for answers: collection of papers presented to a national conference organised by Islington Area Child Protection Committee and the Bridge Child Care Development Service on 1 March 1996 at Church House Conference Centre, London. Pritchard, M. J. The Bridge Child Care Development Service and Islington Area Child Protection Committee.

Keep, G (1996) Going to court: child witnesses in their own words, ChildLine.

Macleod, M and Barter, C (1996) We know it's tough to talk: boys in need of help, ChildLine.

Munro, E. (1996) 'Avoidable and unavoidable mistakes in child protection work', British Journal of Social Work 26; 793-808.

Munro, E. (1999) 'Common errors of reasoning in child protection work', Abuse and Neglect, 23 (8) 745-758.

National Commission of Inquiry into the Prevention of Child Abuse (1996) Childhood Matters: report of the National Commission of Inquiry into the Prevention of Child Abuse, Volume 1: the report, Williams of Mostyn, Lord (Chairman).

NCH Action for Children (1994) Messages from children, children's evaluations of the professional response to child sexual abuse, NCH Action for Children.

Parton, N. (1991). *Governing the Family.* London: Macmillan.

Parton, N. (1996). 'Social work, risk and the blaming system.' in Parton, N. (ed.) *Social Theory, Social Change and Social Work.* London: Routledge.

Phillips, M. 'Issues of ethnicity and culture', in Wilson, K. and James, A. (eds) (1995). The Child Protection Handbook, London: Bailliere Tindall.

Platt, D. (1996) Enquiries and investigations: the policy context, in Platt, D and Shemmings, D. (eds) Making enquiries into alleged child abuse and neglect: partnership with families, John Wiley and Son.

Pringle, K. (1998). *Children and Social Welfare in Europe*. Buckingham: Open University Press.

Roberts, J. and Taylor, C. (1993). 'Sexually abused children and young people speak out', in Waterhouse, L. (ed.) Child Abuse and Child Abusers. London: Jessica Kingsley.

Roberts, J. and Taylor, C. (1999) Sexually abused children speak out in Waterhouse, L. (ed) *Child abuse and child abusers*, Protection and prevention.

Scottish Children's Reporter's Administration (2001) Statistical Bulletin no 24 Referrals of children to Reporters and children's hearings, April.

Scottish Executive (1999) Excluded young people, the report of the Strategy Action Team, Scottish Executive.

Scottish Executive (2000) School meals in education authority schools 1999-2000, National Statistics Publication.

Scottish Executive (2000a) Scottish Partnership on Domestic Abuse, National Strategy to Address Domestic Abuse in Scotland, Scottish Executive.

Scottish Executive (2000b) Protecting children: a collective responsibility – reviewing the contribution of Child Protection Committees to inter-agency co-operation in Scotland: report of a review of Child Protection Committees in Scotland, Scottish Executive.

Scottish Executive (2001) For Scotland's Children Better integrated children's services, Scottish Executive.

Scottish Executive (2001a) Getting our priorities right, police and practice guidelines for working with children and families affected by problem drug use, Scottish Executive.

Scottish Executive (2002) Building a Better Scotland Spending Proposals 2003-2006: What the Money Buys, Scottish Executive.

Scottish Executive (2002) News Release Child Protection Statistics for the Year Ended 31 March 2001, 03 September, Scottish Executive National Statistics Publication.

Scottish Executive Central Research Unit (2002) Disciplining children: research with parents in Scotland, Scottish Executive.

Scottish Women's Aid (1997) Children: Equality and Respect, children and young people's experiences of domestic abuse, Scottish Women's Aid.

Sharland, E. *et al* (1995) Professional intervention in child sexual abuse, HMSO.

Shemmings, D. and Shemmings, Y. (1996) Building trust with families when making enquiries in Platt, D and Shemmings, D. Making enquiries into child abuse and neglect: partnership with families, John Wiley and Sons.

Sinclair, R and Bullock, R. (2002) Learning from past experience – a review of serious case reviews, Department of Health.

Social Service Inspectorate (1997) Messages from inspections, child protection inspections 1992-1996, Department of Health.

Sykes, J. *et al* (2002) Kinship and stranger foster carers, How do they compare? Adoption and Fostering 26, 2, 38-47.

Taylor, C. *et al* (1993) Child Sexual abuse: the child's perspective in Ferguson, H *et al* (eds) Surviving childhood adversity, issues for policy and Practice, Social Studies Press.

Thorburn, J. *et al* (1995) Paternalism or partnership? Family involvement in the child protection process, HMSO.

Waldfogel, J. (2001) *The Future of Child Protection,* Cambridge (Mass.), Harvard University Press.

Waterhouse, L. *et al* (1998) The evaluation of children's hearings in Scotland, Volume 3, Children in Focus, The Scottish Office Central Research Unit.

Wattam, C. (1997) 'Is the criminalisation of child harm and injury in the best interests of the child? Children and Society 11: 97-107.

Westcott, H.L. and Davies, G.M. (1996). 'Sexually abused children's and young people's perspective on investigative interviews.' *British Journal of Social Work* 26: 451-474.

Who Cares? Scotland (undated) Feeling Safe? Report, Who Cares Scotland.

Appendix E

Glossary

Attention Deficit Hyperactivity Disorder (ADHD)	a behavioural disorder in children and young people. Core symptoms include developmentally inappropriate levels of activity and impulsivity and an impaired ability to sustain attention.
Case Conference	where a number of professionals meet to discuss a case that is of concern.
Child	legal classification of person aged under 16 (or under 18 with a current supervision requirement from a children's Hearing).
Child Assessment Order	requires parents or carers to produce a child and allow any assessment needed to take place to help professionals decide whether they should act to safeguard the child's welfare.
Child Protection Committees	monitor and regularly review local inter-agency child protection procedures and help different agencies improve understanding of each others roles and functions in child protection.
Child Protection Order	authorises the applicant to remove a child from circumstances in which he or she is at risk or retain him or her in a place of safety.
Child Protection Plan	agreed inter-agency plan outlining in detail the arrangements for attempting to ensure the protection of a child and supports to the family.
Child Protection Register	a formal list of names of children where there are concerns about the possibility of future abuse and where a child protection plan has been agreed.
Children's Panel	panel of trained lay people to which children who have committed offences, or who are in need of care and protection can be referred.
Children's Hearing	considers the child's behaviour or problems and needs with professionals and families, and makes decisions about what actions to take.

Compulsory Measures of Supervision	statutory arrangements for monitoring and intervening where necessary.
Domestic Abuse	the physical, sexual, and/or mental and emotional abuse of one person, usually a woman, by a partner or ex-partner, usually a man. It can also occur between same-sex partners. Children and young people witness, and are affected by, domestic abuse and there is some correlation between domestic abuse and the physical, sexual and emotional abuse of children.
Emotional Abuse	occurs where there is failure to provide for the child's basic emotional needs such as to have a severe effect on the behaviour and development of the child.
Exclusion Order	requires the removal of a person suspected of harming a child from the family home.
Female Genital Mutilation (FGM)	comprises all procedures involving partial or total removal of the external female genitalia or other injury to the female genital organs whether for cultural or other non-therapeutic reasons.
Foetal Abuse	where a foetus is damaged in utero by acts of omission or commission.
Forced Marriage	a marriage conducted without the valid consent of both parties, where duress is a factor.
'Grounds'	trigger conditions one of which has to be satisfied before a children's Hearing can consider a case.
Institutional Abuse	abuse which takes place in a school or residential setting.
Mandatory Reporting	where professionals are legally required to report their concerns relating to child abuse and neglect.
Neglect	occurs when a child's essential needs are not met and this is likely to cause impairment to physical health and development.
Non-organic Failure to Thrive	can be observed in children who significantly fail to reach normal growth and developmental milestones where physical and genetic reasons have been medically excluded.

Organised Abuse	abuse where there was more than a single abuser and the adults concerned appear to have acted in concert to abuse children and/or where an adult has used an institutional framework or position of authority to recruit children for abuse.
Parent Substitute	an adult either foster carer, relative, family friend or guardian who either formally or informally fulfils the role of a parent for a child.
Peer Abuse	abuse of children and young people by other children or young people.
Physical Abuse	actual or attempted physical injury to a child where there is definite knowledge or reasonable suspicion that the injury was inflicted or knowingly not prevented.
Procurator Fiscal	public prosecutor who, following the reporting of a crime, decides whether or not to prosecute.
Racial Abuse	where a person is subjected to racial attacks or harassment.
Reporter	an independent person, employed by the Scottish Children's Reporters Administration who has statutory powers for the protection and wellbeing of all children, wide discretionary powers and a large measure of independence. When the Reporter receives information that a child may be in need of compulsory measures of supervision, he or she must make any further enquiries he or she considers necessary before deciding either to take no further action, to refer the child to the social work department for voluntary assistance or to refer to a children's Hearing.
Risk Assessment	the process of assessing the risk caused or faced by an individual and how much harm is likely to result if the risks are realised.
Schedule 1 Offenders	offenders convicted of offences against children. This includes sexual and violent offences.
Self-harming	behaviour by children or young people where they deliberately harm themselves, most commonly by inflicting cuts on their body, starving or overdosing with drink or drugs.

Appendix E

Sexual Abuse	actual or threatened sexual assault or exploitation of a child or adult victim.
Sudden Infant Death Syndrome (SIDS)	the sudden and unexpected death of a baby for no obvious reason, that remains unexplained after post-mortem examination. Also know as cot death.
Supervision Requirement	places a child under the supervision of the local authority.
System Abuse	where the operation of legislation, officially sanctioned procedures or operational policies within systems or institutions are avoidably damaging to children and their families.
United Nations Convention on the Rights of the Child	an international human rights treaty which articulates the human rights for children and standards to which governments must aspire in realising these rights.
Young Offender	legal classification of offender aged from 16 to 21.